KD
7876
.S5x

016168

Shoolbred, Claude Frederick.
   The administration of criminal
justice in England and Wales / C. F.
Shoolbred; foreword by Harold B.
Williams. Oxford, New York [etc.] :
Pergamon, 1966.
   xxiii, 158 p. : ill., tables. ; 20
cm. (Commonwealth and international
library)
   Pergamon modern legal outlines.

   1. Criminal justice, Administration
of--Great Britain. I. Title

13 SEP 85   887672   OMMMxc   66-16882

THE COMMONWEALTH AND INTERNATIONAL LIBRARY

Joint Chairmen of the Honorary Editorial Advisory Board
SIR ROBERT ROBINSON, O.M., F.R.S., LONDON
DEAN ATHELSTAN SPILHAUS, MINNESOTA
Publisher: ROBERT MAXWELL, M.C., M.P.

PERGAMON MODERN LEGAL OUTLINES
General Editor: W. A. J. FARNDALE

The Administration of Criminal Justice in England and Wales

The Administration of Criminal Justice in England and Wales

BY

C. F. SHOOLBRED, B.A., LL.B. (Cantab.)

of the Middle Temple, Barrister-at-Law
Clerk of the Peace for the Middlesex Area of Greater London

Author of Lotteries and the Law and
The Law of Gaming and Betting

FOREWORD BY

HAROLD B. WILLIAMS, Q.C., LL.D.

PERGAMON PRESS

OXFORD · LONDON · EDINBURGH · NEW YORK
TORONTO · PARIS · BRAUNSCHWEIG

Pergamon Press Ltd., Headington Hill Hall, Oxford
4 & 5 Fitzroy Square, London W.1

Pergamon Press (Scotland) Ltd., 2 & 3 Teviot Place, Edinburgh 1

Pergamon Press Inc., 44-01 21st Street, Long Island City, New York 11101

Pergamon of Canada, Ltd., 6 Adelaide Street East, Toronto, Ontario

Pergamon Press S.A.R.L., 24 rue des Écoles, Paris, 5ᵉ

Vieweg & Sohn GmbH, Burgplatz 1, 33 Braunschweig

Copyright © 1966 Pergamon Press Ltd.
First edition 1966
Library of Congress Catalog Card No. 66–16882

Printed in Great Britain by Vellum Samson Printers Ltd., Parkstone, Poole, Dorset

KD
7876
.S5x

This book is sold subject to the condition
that it shall not, by way of trade, be lent,
resold, hired out, or otherwise disposed
of without the publisher's consent,
in any form of binding or cover
other than that in which
it is published.

(2751/66)

Contents

Foreword by HAROLD B. WILLIAMS, Q.C., LL.D.   vii

Preface   xv

Introduction   xix

Table of Courts Engaged in Administering Criminal Law   xxiii

1   MAGISTRATES' COURTS   1

Appointment of magistrates — Size of the bench — Justices' clerks — Summary trial — Plea of guilty in absence of accused — Trial of information — Power of adjournment — Hearing at magistrates' court — Offences triable summarily or on indictment — Committal to Quarter Sessions for sentence — Committal for trial — Vagrancy — Juvenile courts — Affiliation orders — Domestic proceedings — Licensing — Bookmaker's permit and betting office licence — Civil debts

2   TRANSITION FROM MAGISTRATES' COURTS TO QUARTER SESSIONS AND ASSIZE COURTS   22

Committal for trial — Depositions — Committals for sentence — Indictments — *Nolle prosequi* — Fixing of dates — Arrangements of lists — Appeals — Calendars — County day agenda

3   JURORS   43

Precept — Jury panel — Jury excuses — Empanelling juries — Penalty for non-appearance — Challenge to jurors — Putting in charge — Considering verdict — Communications to judge or chairman — Taking of verdict — Payment of jurors

4 TRIAL BY JURY — QUARTER SESSIONS 63

Pleas of guilty — Pleas of not guilty — Adjournments — Witnesses — Exhibits — Judgement of the court — Bail estreats — Additional cases taken into consideration — Corrective training and preventive detention — Quarter Sessions: Size of bench, Rota of justices, Applications to court, Breaches of probation orders and conditional discharges, Committals for sentence, Appeals from magistrates' courts, Licensing

5 AFTER-TRIAL DUTIES—APPEALS TO COURT OF CRIMINAL APPEAL 104

Committal warrants — Estreat roll — Return to Treasury of fines — After-trial calendar — Notices to clerks to justices — Witness and juror expenses — Costs in criminal cases — Legal aid certificates — Examination of bills of costs — Appeals to Court of Criminal Appeal — Appeals to the House of Lords

APPENDIX I. Recent Statutes affecting Criminal Procedure 135

APPENDIX II. Dictionary of Prison Slang 139

APPENDIX III. Glossary of Legal Terms in Criminal Law 141

Table of Statutes 147

Index 153

Foreword

IT IS a pleasure to me to write a foreword to Mr. Shoolbred's book. As deputy chairman of the court I was constantly associated with him for some years in the work of Middlesex Sessions and therefore had ample opportunity to become acquainted with his immense knowledge of the law and the practice regulating the conduct of courts of criminal jurisdiction.

The criminal courts of this country, from the magistrates' courts to the Court of Criminal Appeal, are the inheritors and guardians of a great tradition, and are responsible for handing on that tradition to their successors. Phrased with complete economy of language, that tradition is that persons accused in our courts are entitled to a fair trial. Phrased in more legal language it is that no one should be convicted of a criminal offence unless the court or a jury is sure that the offence has been proved by the evidence beyond reasonable doubt. On this tradition, now enshrined in our law, our liberties as Englishmen depend.

It is provocative of thought that the organization of our system of courts has undergone little substantial alteration in 600 years. Practically all offences are presented in the first instance to a magistrates' court, where the allegations against the accused are considered, and if a prima facie case is established, and the case is not one with which the magistrates can deal themselves, the accused is committed to Assizes, the Central Criminal Court, or a court of Quarter Sessions for trial. The rules of evidence and procedure and the consequences to the accused of a verdict of guilty have changed over the centuries, as has the judge's influence on the jury. We feel a justifiable pride in the extent to which our system of justice has spread over the world, throughout what is now the Commonwealth and what is now the United States of America. It is no less a matter of pride that in the interpretation of the common law the opinions, for example, of the Supreme Court of the United States and of the High Court of Australia have high persuasive authority in our courts.

One of the foundations of our liberties is that no inhabitant of these islands can be imprisoned or otherwise punished for an indictable offence, except on his own confession, unless twelve of his fellows think it right that it should be so. We take this for granted, forgetting perhaps that it was a hard-won liberty and that in times best forgotten many jurors were imprisoned before the principle was established

The duties of a court in ensuring the administration of justice according to law extend to each of the five matters which Mr. Shoolbred has made the subject of his chapters. The court has to consider matters occurring before the trial, for example the regularity of any interrogation of the accused having regard to the "Judges' Rules", recently amended, and the admissibility of evidence as to which the court has a discretion.

The "Judges' Rules" are a guide to discretion. Judges control the conduct of trials and the admission of evidence against persons on trial before them. They do not supervise the police, but it is the law of England that statements made by an accused person are only admissible in evidence if they are voluntary in the sense that they have not been obtained from him by fear of prejudice or hope of advantage exercised or held out by a person in authority or by oppression. Police officers are entitled to question any person, whether suspected or not, from whom they think that useful information may be obtained, whether or not that person has been taken into custody so long as he has not been charged with the offence or informed that he may be prosecuted, but if there are reasonable grounds for suspecting that a person has committed an offence, a caution must be given before any further questions are put.

These rules do not affect the principle that it is the duty of every citizen to help the police to discover and apprehend offenders.

During a trial objection is from time to time taken to the admissibility of a statement said to have been made, verbally or in writing, by an accused person. This results in what is often called "a trial within a trial". In the absence of the jury the presiding judge will hear evidence from the police officers concerned and from the accused as to the circumstances in which the statement was made and what was in fact said. In his discretion he will then decide whether the statement is admissible in whole or in part, and only after his decision has been given are the jury readmitted to the court.

In the course of their investigations the police may have taken statements from other people, some of whom may be called as witnesses. These statements may not be given in evidence, and verbal evidence may not be given as to what was said unless the statements were made in the presence of the accused and in his hearing.

The court has duties in respect of juries. I have read with interest and sympathy Mr. Shoolbred's observations on this subject. No one with any responsibility for the administration of justice can fail to feel anxiety about it. Mr. Shoolbred's experience of the County of Middlesex began when jurors might expect to discharge their duty in one day, albeit a long one. They must now face continuous, or almost continuous, attendance for 3 weeks, possibly more. It is true that in modern times this duty is unlikely to fall on any individual more than once or twice in a lifetime, but it is a serious matter, for example, to the proprietor of a one-man business. Indeed, it is serious to most jurors. I am glad to take the opportunity of acknowledging the very great interest which jurors take in their duties and their appreciation of the importance of those duties. They make some mistakes, as we all do, especially in their first case, when in their anxiety to do right they sometimes acquit when they should not. This is the price of liberty, and I find it refreshing to observe that

I have only once known a jury to convict in a case which I did not think was proved beyond reasonable doubt. After all, they may have been right.

Mr. Shoolbred's account of the trial will be found instructive. The empanelling of a jury is important. It is open to doubt whether the right to challenge jurors without cause shown is worth preserving. Some defendants, especially motorists, seem to have an objection to trial by women, and will challenge every woman on a jury. In the case of an experienced jury which has worked happily together for a week or more, this may well be a short cut to conviction, but the practice persists.

The power of the judge or chairman to direct the empanelling of a jury of men only, or of women only, as the case may require, is important. I have found counsel hesitate to apply for such an order, but in certain cases of gross indecency between male persons it is proper to order a jury composed of men only, and Mr. Shoolbred reminds us that the judge or chairman may so order at his own instance.

The rather complicated provisions which now deal with the punishment of young offenders are carefully dealt with, and Mr. Shoolbred draws attention to the advantage, in certain cases, of committing young offenders under section 29 of the Criminal Justice Act, 1948.

Committals for sentence provide a most important part of the functions of Quarter Sessions, and it is well to be reminded, as Mr. Shoolbred reminds us, of the great assistance the court has in this duty. The police officer in charge of the case gives the prisoner's antecedents, a probation officer in a majority of cases presents a report, the Home Office report as to the prisoner's suitability for certain types of punishment, and in proper cases the court has reports from one or more medical officers.

This assistance is also available after a conviction by a jury. When an accused person intends to plead "not guilty" it is not the practice of probation officers to discuss the matter with him pending trial, and rightly so. But if the court, after conviction,

Foreword

feels that such a report would be of advantage, the consideration of sentence will be postponed for a time in order that a report may be presented. This is wholly to the prisoner's advantage. If he is not given the advantage of probation the period during which he is in custody will count as part of his sentence.

The primary duty of the court is to punish the offender so that the public may be protected, but in considering sentences it is obviously right that everything which tells in favour of the accused, or which may mitigate the seriousness of the offence, is present to the mind of the court, and it is equally right that the accused should know what is said and that he or his counsel be given an opportunity of cross-examining the witness on the evidence. Some people seem to think that each type of offence should carry a uniform sentence. This is nonsense. There are many matters to consider, and the decision as to what is right is one that gives constant anxiety to judges and to chairmen of sessions and the magistrates who are their colleagues. It is probably a rare happening that two consecutive sentences for the same offence are identical.

Books could be written on the subject of sentencing and, indeed, have been. There seems in modern times to be a tendency to suggest that psychiatrists or persons with other forms of experience are better qualified than experienced judges to decide what is appropriate. It is even, I think, thought that the criminal tendency is a form of disease and that curative treatment should replace punishment. This is not wholly nonsense, but it is a view capable of exaggeration, and one cannot help feeling that education and training should eliminate this tendency to wrongdoing, to which most of us in youth would tend if not corrected. Most experienced judges have difficulty in accepting the view that a crime has been committed because the accused could not help it. I have an uneasy feeling that there are two classes of offence — indecent exposure by men and shoplifting by women — which are often capable of no other explanation. I have myself had to decide what to do with an elderly offender of the former class with 300 previous convictions. There is only one answer, but one is left with the hope that in the course of the inevitable imprisonment some attempt will be made to help. It need hardly be added that a total of 300 convictions involves necessary criticism of the sentencing courts.

It is impossible to prescribe general rules as to sentencing. The guidance recently given by Parliament, and the proposal now made to abolish short sentences, have made — and if enacted will make — the task of judges more and more difficult. It is quite certain that a young man, who has perhaps been given the benefit of probation and perhaps been fined, is more likely to learn a salutary lesson from a short sentence of imprisonment, not exceeding 6 months, than in any other way. That is one reason why detention centres, with a normal sentence of 3 months, are so successful. But apart from that problem, the determination of the appropriate sentence is perhaps the gravest responsibility which falls upon a judge. The history of this subject in our country, as in all others, is one of slowness to temper justice with mercy. King Ini wrote, a thousand years ago, "In general let mild punishments be decreed, for the people's need, and let not for a little God's image and His own handywork be destroyed, which He so dearly bought". Long after those words were written, people were hanged in this country for trumpery thefts. I have spoken of the value of a short, sharp sentence at the beginning of what might be a life of crime, but there will always remain the problem of the mature and persistent offender, and the question which every judge must ask himself "Is it too late?" Sometimes it is. Sometimes the possibility of self-help, on which, after all, reform depends, has gone, and the only life with which a man is content is that of prison. Cases occur in which it may be a judge's duty to send a man of 70 to prison for 10 years. It is probably true that on the passing of such a sentence there are two people in court — the judge and the prisoner — who know that it is right. Those are cases in which it is, unhappily, too late. But it is not so uncommon as might be supposed to find a man awaiting sentence who has served many terms of imprisonment and has never been given a chance. In these days of probation and after-care it may well be that it is not too late. The judge must weigh his duty to the public with the desire which he must feel to help a human being. Judges are human and find it a wonderful thing to get letters from such people who have, after all, made good.

Mr. Shoolbred deals at length with the duties of the court of Quarter Sessions and its clerk in respect of appeals. The appellate jurisdiction of Quarter Sessions is of great importance. When a person is convicted in a magistrates' court and appeals to Quarter Sessions, there is no appeal against conviction to the Court of Criminal Appeal, though there is power in the Queen's Bench Division to review the decision, if there be error in law, by order of certiorari.

The work involved is increasing. Recently figures were published of the increasing number of indictable offences known to the police. The figures need not be repeated in full. It is sufficient to say that the total has grown from 283,000 in 1938 to 1,066,467 in 1964. These are frightening figures. They cover the whole period of the modern development of the welfare state, and reach a period when no crime need be committed to avoid starvation. Parliament a few years ago relieved Quarter Sessions of a considerable volume of work in cases of breaking and entering by empowering magistrates' courts to deal with these cases (other than housebreaking). But the right of the accused to trial by jury remains, as does the right of appeal.

Motoring cases also provide an increasing volume of appellate work. Cases of driving under the influence of drink or drugs, or of dangerous driving, are often committed for trial at Sessions in the first instance, but even if they are not, there is still the right of appeal.

Still more, perhaps, is the increase of work due to the increasing number of cases dealt with by magistrates' courts.

No figures are available of the number of days on which

criminal courts sit in this country, but it is a large number. With certain limited exceptions, and subject to certain powers to prohibit the publication of certain facts, our law requires that this jurisdiction be exercised in public, with open doors, and protects newspapers in regard to the publication of fair and accurate reports, though no doubt pressure on space prevents publication of more than a minute fraction of the total number of cases. In every month of the year judges of the Queen's Bench Division travel the country to hold the Assizes, and in many counties courts of Quarter Sessions sit almost daily throughout the year. And the increase continues.

An understanding of the work of the criminal courts is therefor of public importance. This book deals with the functions of all the criminal courts of this country. It is impossible to read the book without an appreciation of the immense volume of work which falls upon these courts and of the great responsibility which rests upon them. On the discharge of that responsibility in accordance with law, our liberties as Englishmen depend.

HAROLD B. WILLIAMS

Preface

I HAVE often thought when sitting in court how strange the whole proceedings must seem to those who are summoned, often for the first time in their lives, either to act as jurors or to go through the ordeal of giving evidence from the witness box. Judges, chairmen of quarter sessions, and barristers are themselves so steeped in the ways of the courts that very little consideration is given to this factor. One of the purposes, therefore, that I have in mind in writing this manual is to try to set out in simple language what takes place in our courts. In order to assist those readers who may be unfamiliar with legal terms, a glossary of such terms has been added in Appendix III, reference to which will, it is hoped, assist to better understanding of the text. If by so doing I succeed in giving a small insight to some people, who are thereby made a little less nervous of the strange surroundings into which they find themselves suddenly plunged, then the effort of producing this treatise will have fully justified itself.

There is also the possibility that I may succeed in being of at least some assistance not only to all those many persons throughout the length and breadth of the land who are closely associated with the most interesting work of the administration of justice, but also to all those students whose future careers are destined to be devoted to a direct participation in this work, either as practising barristers or solicitors or as members of the staffs of Assize courts, clerks of the peace, or justices' clerks.

The Criminal Justice Act, 1948, had as one of its main objectives the amendment of the law relating to the procedure of criminal courts, including the law relating to evidence before such courts. Between the operative date of that Act and the present time, several other statutes having an important bearing upon criminal procedure have been enacted.

The cumulative effect of all these Acts has been to add materially to the work of the courts. The jurisdiction of both Petty Sessions and of Quarter Sessions, for instance, has been enlarged. This manual is not intended to be a textbook, and whilst it is necessary to cite many statutes it is not intended to quote any authorities. Specific reference will be made to the many and varied duties which have to be undertaken by clerks of assizes, clerks of the peace, and their staffs.

The motorist may be taken as an example, in order to illustrate the tremendous increase that has taken place during the past few decades in the number of people whose lives have become affected in one way or another by the administration of justice. Reference has only to be made to speed limits, parking meters, and other minor infringements of the motoring laws, in order to mention only a few of the possible pitfalls into which an otherwise law-abiding citizen may fall, to illustrate the fact that an ever-increasing number of persons find themselves unwilling victims of the long arm of the law.

Two other factors also have to be borne in mind. First, that as the number of prosecutions increase, so of necessity must the number of persons who are called to give evidence, either on behalf of the prosecution or for the defence, become more numerous. Secondly, with the inevitable rise in the number of cases resulting from more prosecutions, it follows that the work of Assizes and Quarter Sessions also gets much heavier. It is at these courts that many citizens get caught up in the net of jury service.

The past three decades may be said to have revolutionized the work of the courts in this country. Two main factors have had a bearing on this. First, the large number of important statutes bearing on criminal administration which have found their way on to the Statute Book during that period, serving in most instances either to increase the jurisdiction of magistrates' courts or Quarter Sessions, or both. Secondly, there has been an enormous increase in the size of the calendars at Assizes and Quarter Sessions together with an enormous expansion in the number of cases dealt with at the lower courts.

An incidental matter which arises out of the activity of Parliament in this respect is the fact that quite often the statutes which affect the work of the courts are brought into operation piecemeal. The medium for bringing certain sections into operation on one date and others on a subsequent date or dates is that of Statutory Rules and Regulations. The net result is that an ever-watchful eye has to be kept on these Acts which have received the Queen's assent.

A further factor which follows as of course, is the increase in crime generally. The busier the magistrates' courts become so, it follows, do the courts of Assize and Quarter Sessions. In some ways Quarter Sessions have tended to have a heavier increase since Assize courts have sought relief from the enormous increase of work and as a result more cases are being committed for trial to Quarter Sessions.

The magistrates' courts and Quarter Sessions, and to some extent the Assize courts, have all found a big increase in their work during recent years by reason of the number of motoring offences with which they have to deal. Quarter Sessions which deal with appeals by defendants who have been convicted by magistrates have found that more and more time is taken up by such cases, besides having to deal with a larger influx of trial cases.

It might be of interest in passing to note that during the year 1938 Middlesex Quarter Sessions dealt with 461 prisoners arising from 296 cases, whereas in the year 1962 those sessions dealt with no less than 1273 prisoners arising from 945 cases. The July calendar of those sessions in 1938 consisted of 37 prisoners arising from 23 cases for trial, whereas in July 1963 there were 202 prisoners arising from 156 cases.

Similar figures showing the enormous increase in the work of Quarter Sessions generally throughout the whole country could doubtless be produced, and merely serve to illustrate the way in which the work has tended to increase.

In May 1963 a Departmental Committee under the chairmanship of the Right Honourable Lord Morris of Borth-y-Gest, C.B.E., M.C., was appointed by the Secretary of State for Home Affairs, to inquire into the law and practice in England and Wales regarding the qualifications for, exemptions from, and conditions of jury service and related matters, and to make recommendations. Since, however, it is likely to be some time before such recommendations are made, and even longer before they are implemented, no reference is made in the chapter on jurors to this Departmental Committee.

The author wishes to express his sincere thanks to Mr. Fitzwalter Butler, Chairman of the South-East Area Quarter Sessions of Greater London, for his most thorough and careful editing of the text, as also, for the many valuable suggestions he has put forward during this careful survey; to Mr. W. W. Hickman, former Chief Sessions Clerk at Middlesex Quarter Sessions, for giving in full measure the benefit of his many years of experience in the work of both petty sessional courts and at Quarter Sessions; and also to Mr. Harold Williams, Q.C., LL.D., for kindly consenting to write a foreword.

C. F. S.

Introduction

BROADLY speaking, the administration of justice in this country is on a three-tier basis — magistrates' courts, Quarter Sessions, and Assizes. The vast majority of cases are in fact dealt with at magistrates' courts, the great majority of which are manned by lay justices. There are some stipendiary magistrates in the larger towns and the metropolitan magistrates in the London area.

The fundamental difference between trials in magistrates' courts and trials at Quarter Sessions or Assizes is that the former take place before a bench of magistrates (or a stipendiary or metropolitan magistrate, as the case may be) whilst trials at Quarter Sessions or Assizes are trials by jury.

The jurisdiction of magistrates' courts is not so great as that of Quarter Sessions, whilst the jurisdiction of Assizes is the highest of all. There are three main ways in which a magistrates' court does its work. First, there are minor cases which can be tried only by such a court. Secondly, there are cases in which the defendant has the right to elect to go for trial by jury, although the magistrates have the necessary jurisdiction to try the case themselves. It is the duty of the magistrates' clerk in such cases to advise the defendant of his right to elect trial by jury.

In a similar category are a number of cases in which either the prosecution or the defence have the right to elect trial by jury. In certain cases the magistrates themselves have the right, although they have started to try a case themselves, to break off and treat the case as one for trial by jury.

The third type of case is that in which the magistrates' sole function is to make sure that there is a prima facie case made out by the prosecution for the defence to answer. In this event the evidence of the witnesses is taken down by the magistrates' clerk in the form of what are known as depositions. The case is then committed to Quarter Sessions or Assizes, as the case may be, for trial.

A person who has been convicted at a magistrates' court has a right of appeal, if he pleaded guilty against his sentence, or, if he pleaded not guilty, against both his conviction and sentence. On a point of law a person convicted by the magistrates can go to the High Court by what is known as a "case stated". Similarly, a person who is convicted at Quarter Sessions or Assizes has a right of appeal to the Court of Criminal Appeal.

The magistrates' courts have the assistance of Stone's *Justices Manual*, whilst Quarter Sessions and the Assize courts have as their main textbook that most valuable guide known as Archbold's *Criminal Pleading, Evidence and Practice*.

There is, however, so far as I am aware, no book for reference having as its main objective the compilation and explanation of the various and essential duties which are necessary to the administration of justice. If one takes, for example, the many and varied duties of a clerk of the peace, the knowledge that is required to carry out such duties efficiently is in large measure handed down by word of mouth or duly acquired in the hard school of practical experience.

It is proposed to divide this manual into the following chapters. Chapter 1 will deal with magistrates' courts and set out some of the work that is done at these courts in a general way. Chapter 2 will be by way of transition and illustrate the link between the petty sessional courts and the trial courts of Quarter Sessions and Assizes. Chapter 3 will deal with the very human subject of jurors, which the author considers warrants a chapter to itself; especially as it is in this respect that it may be possible to render some assistance to the many members of the public who are likely to be summoned to do their duty as jurors. Then in

Introduction

Chapter 4 a more detailed account of trial and other work at Assizes and Quarter Sessions will be given.

Chapter 5 deals with the important subject of after-trial duties. This chapter also takes the reader a stage further along the administration of justice by referring to the process of appeal to the Court of Criminal Appeal.

An appendix (Appendix II) setting out a dictionary of prison slang has been added and may be of interest, together with an appendix (Appendix III) setting out a glossary of legal terms used in criminal law.

Thus the reader will be taken through the courts starting with summary jurisdiction, passing on to trial by jury and then to what, for all practical purposes, is the final court of appeal as regards crime.

It will be appreciated that since the procedure in the courts at Assizes is similar to that at Quarter Sessions, it is not necessary to devote a separate chapter to Assize courts. The important difference between the two courts is, of course, that whilst the jurisdiction of Quarter Sessions is restricted to dealing with certain cases, there are no such restrictions with regard to the Assize courts.

Modern legislation has introduced so many technicalities in the administration of justice that it is no easy matter for new recruits to the courts to be trained. It is safe to say that "a little knowledge is a dangerous thing". The staffs of most courts are nowadays so busy sitting in court that frequently junior members have to be left in the general office to deal with the many and varied streams of callers who come seeking information. Another possible danger is the telephone; great care has to be taken to ensure that only correct advice is supplied.

It is sufficient to cite such recent landmarks of criminal administration as the Administration of Justice (Miscellaneous Provisions) Act, 1933, the Children and Young Persons Acts, 1933 to 1963, the Criminal Justice Acts, 1948, 1961, and 1962, the Road Traffic Acts, 1930, 1960, and 1962, the Magistrates'

Courts Acts, 1952 and 1957, the Mental Health Act, 1959, the Licensing Acts, 1961 and 1964, and the Betting and Gaming Acts, 1960 and 1963, all of which have considerable bearing on the work of the criminal courts of this country, in order to appreciate some of the extra duties and responsibilities that have been imposed on these courts.

One of the most fascinating aspects of work connected with the administration of justice is, to my mind, the variety of the work. One has only to look at a list of daily cases for hearing at a magistrates' court or a calendar of cases for trial at an Assize or Quarter Sessions, to realize the wide number of different offences with which the courts are called upon to deal in the course of their daily routine.

Courts Engaged in Administering Criminal Law

Court	Bench	Court official	Matters dealt with
Magistrates'	Chairman and lay justices Stipendiary magistrates	Justices' clerk	Summary trials Preliminary hearings prior to committal for trial at Quarter Sessions or Assizes
Juvenile	Chairman and lay justices	Justices' clerk	Charges against children and young persons
Quarter Sessions	Chairman and lay justices. Extended jurisdiction when salaried and qualified chairman presides	Clerk of the peace	Trials by jury. Sentencing of persons committed from petty sessional courts. Hearing of appeals from magistrates' courts
Divisional Court of The High Court of Justice (Queen's Bench Division)	High Court judges	Associate of the High Court	Appeals on points of law from decisions by magistrates' courts or Quarter Sessions
Assizes	High Court judges and Commissioners of Assize	Clerk of assize	Trial by jury of more serious charges not triable by Quarter Sessions, i.e. murder and manslaughter
Criminal Appeal	High court judges	Registrar of Court of Criminal Appeal	Appeals from Quarter Sessions and Assizes
House of Lords	Law lords	Registrar of the Clerk of the Parliaments	Appeals from the Court of Criminal Appeal

CHAPTER 1

Magistrates' Courts

Appointments of magistrates — Size of the Bench — Justices' clerks — Summary trial — Plea of guilty in absence of accused — Trial of information — Power of adjournment — Hearing at magistrates' court — Offences triable summarily or on indictment — Committal to Quarter Sessions for sentence — Committal for trial — Vagrancy — Juvenile courts — Affiliation orders — Domestic proceedings — Licensing — Bookmaker's permit and betting office licence — Civil debts

THE first stage to be considered in dealing with the administration of justice in this country is the work of the magistrates' courts. In this chapter, therefore, it is proposed to touch lightly on the various duties undertaken by those courts without going into too much detail.

APPOINTMENT OF MAGISTRATES

In ancient times magistrates used to be known as conservatores of the peace, and it was not until the year 1361 that the title of Justice of the Peace was introduced by the Justices of the Peace Act of that year. In modern times justices of the peace are appointed by the Crown. Recommendations are made through the medium of the *custos rotulorum* (usually the Lord Lieutenant of the County, but not necessarily so), by local advisory committees which are appointed by the Lord Chancellor to inform him and advise him in this matter. Every magistrate on his appointment is enrolled on the county commission and has to take the oath of allegiance and the judicial oath before he can undertake his duties as a justice of the peace.

A justice shall not be qualified to sit as a member of a juvenile court unless he is a member of a juvenile panel, that is to say, a panel of justices specially qualified to deal with juvenile cases. A juvenile court panel has to be formed for every petty sessions area.

The Justices (Supplemental List) Rules, 1950, which came into operation on the 1st June 1950, laid a duty on the clerk of the peace or other officer having the custody of the commission to enter in the Supplemental List kept for that county or borough the name of any person appointed a Justice of Commission on his attaining the age of 75 years. The Lord Chancellor may also direct the name of a justice to be so entered, or give approval for this to be done whether of that age or not.

SIZE OF THE BENCH

The Justices of the Peace (Size and Chairmanship of Bench) Rules, 1950, which came into force on the 1st January 1951, laid down that the number of county or borough justices sitting to deal with a case at a magistrates' court shall not be greater than seven. In spite of this provision, however, the Lord Chancellor has intimated that only in special circumstances should more than five justices sit on a petty sessional bench at the same time.

The pressure of work since these Rules came into force has, however, resulted in most magistrates' courts having to convene more and more courts, with the result that the magistrates' courts, far from being able to attain this quota, are often hard put to it to find the requisite number of magistrates in order to satisfy the necessary minimum.

When, however, the proceedings are a preliminary investigation with a view to committal for trial by a jury, then the functions of examining justices may be discharged by a single justice.

The above-mentioned restrictions apply only to magistrates'

courts which are manned by lay justices. A stipendiary magistrate is empowered to sit by himself.

In the event, therefore, of any petty sessional area finding that it is short of effective magistrates, it is the duty of the clerk to the justices to make the necessary representations to the Advisory Committee with a view to more appointments being made to the Commission in order to add to the strength of his bench.

The Magistrates' Courts Act, 1952, in conjunction with the Magistrates' Courts Rules, 1952, are now the main instruments on which the administration of the law at magistrates' courts is based. The Act is a consolidation of several old statutes and deals comprehensively with the practice and proceedings before magistrates courts and the functions of justices' clerks and matters connected therewith.

The criminal jurisdiction of magistrates' courts can be divided into three main categories, that is to say, summary trial of informations or complaints, the trial of offences which are triable on indictment or summarily, and preliminary hearings to determine whether there is a prima facie case on which to commit a defendant to an Assize court or to Quarter Sessions for trial by jury.

Another way of expressing this is to say that summary cases are those in which a defendant has no right to be tried by a jury. Regarding the second category — cases triable summarily or on indictment by a jury — certain conditions have to be observed in order to determine which procedure is adopted. The third category, preliminary hearings of cases which are triable only on indictment by a jury, can, of course, be dealt with only in that way.

JUSTICES' CLERKS

Having seen how magistrates are appointed, let us now deal with the appointment of the principal officer of those courts, namely the justices' clerk. The Justices of the Peace Act, 1949, is the modern statute which deals with these appointments and generally regulates the administration of magistrates' courts. It was this Act which brought into being Magistrates' Courts Committees and enacted that there shall be a Magistrates' Court Committee for each county and for each county borough.

Justices' clerks, whose duties, broadly speaking, include advising the magistrates on law and undertaking the whole responsibility for the various administrative duties which have to be performed in a magistrates' court, are appointed by and hold office at the pleasure of the Magistrates' Courts Committee created by the Justices of the Peace Act, 1949, for these courts.

A justices' clerk is now by virtue of his office the collecting officer of any court of summary jurisdiction of which he is the clerk, and as such has to discharge all functions conferred by any enactment on a collecting officer under the Affiliation Orders Act, 1914. Furthermore, a justices' clerk is also responsible for the administration of any order for periodical payments made by a magistrates' court. This duty is now enacted in section 52 of the Magistrates' Courts Act, 1952, and the Magistrates' Courts Rules 32 and 33.

The main functions of such committees are to appoint justices' clerks and their staff, to submit to the Secretary of State from time to time draft orders concerning the division of the county or any part thereof into petty sessional divisions, and to make provision for courses of instruction for justices of their area; which matter is subject to the approval of the Lord Chancellor.

SUMMARY TRIAL

Section 98 of the Magistrates' Courts Act, 1952, lays down that a magistrates' court shall not try an information summarily or hear a complaint except when composed of at least two justices. unless the trial or hearing is one that by virtue of any enactment may take place before a single justice. An example of the latter is to be found in the powers given to justices regarding the punishment of rogues and vagabonds under section 4 of the Vagrancy Act, 1824. Whilst conviction by one justice restricts the power of punishment to a period not exceeding 14 days imprisonment, two justices are empowered to impose a period of imprisonment not exceeding 3 months. Similarly, one justice is limited to imposing a fine of £1, whereas two justices may impose a fine up to the limit of £25 (Magistrates' Courts Act, 1952, section 27 (3)).

PLEA OF GUILTY IN ABSENCE OF ACCUSED

The Magistrates' Courts Act, 1957, which was an Act to make provision for persons charged with certain summary offences to plead guilty, without having to appear in court in person, was enacted with a view to relieving the congestion of minor cases in the courts and also to save persons so charged the inconvenience of having to attend court in person.

Broadly speaking, the provisions of this Act enable a person against whom a summons has been issued requiring him to appear before a magistrates' court, other than a juvenile court, not being (a) an offence which is also triable on indictment, or (b) an offence for which the accused is liable to be sentenced to be imprisoned for a term exceeding 3 months, subject to certain conditions being fulfilled, to have the case heard and disposed of by the magistrates in his absence.

Provision is also made in section 3 of the Act for proving previous convictions in the absence of the accused. It should be noted, however, that the provisions of the above Act only apply to minor infringements of the law such as parking offences or alleged breaches of speed limits.

At this point it may be of assistance to set out the recommended form as approved by the Home Office, which a person who desires to plead guilty without attending the magistrates' court should use.

To the Clerk of the ... Magistrates' Court

Plea of guilty

I have read the Statement(s) of Facts relating to the charge(s) of ... which is/are to be heard by the Magistrates' court on ... I plead guilty to the charge(s) and I desire that the court should dispose of the case in my absence. I wish to bring to the court's attention the mitigating circumstances set out below.

Signed..............................

In such cases the prosecution is strictly confined to reading the statement without any addition or alteration thereto.

TRIAL OF INFORMATION

The information shall state the name of the party charged, and the offence, together with the place when and where the offence is alleged to have been committed

If the accused appears in person, the court shall state to him the substance of the information and ask him whether he pleads guilty or not guilty. These necessary preliminaries are carried out by the clerk to the justices.

After hearing the evidence and the parties, the court shall convict the accused or dismiss the information.

In the event of the accused pleading guilty, the court may convict him without hearing evidence. It has, however, to be borne in mind that justices can proceed to a conviction only if the defendant unambiguously admits the allegation made against him, after the offence with which he is charged has been fully brought to his notice. The importance of great care being taken to ascertain that the accused's plea is genuinely one of guilty lies in the fact that the accused's right of appeal is affected thereby.

An accused person who pleads not guilty and is found guilty and sentenced by the magistrates has the right to appeal to Quarter Sessions against both his conviction and sentence, or against either, at his discretion; but where he has pleaded guilty his right of appeal is restricted to sentence only.

Therefore, if an appellant raises the point that he did not plead guilty in a completely unambiguous way, as for example, a plea of guilty to receiving but not knowing the article in question was stolen; this point will have to be determined as a preliminary issue by Quarter Sessions; and in the event of that court coming to the conclusion that the accused's plea was not in fact clear and unambiguous, the court is empowered to remit the case back to the magistrates with a direction to hear the matter on the basis that the appellant pleaded not guilty.

Should the magistrates then convict, it is open to the accused to appeal to Quarter Sessions against both his conviction and sentence in the ordinary way.

Apart from certain statutory exceptions, an information must be laid within 6 months from the time when the offence was committed or the matter of complaint arose.

Speaking generally, the burden of proof rests on the prosecution. One example of an exception to this general rule is in offences regarding aliens when the burden is on the accused to prove that on the balance of probabilities he is not in fact alien but a British subject.

POWER OF ADJOURNMENT

A magistrates' court may at any time, whether before or after starting to try an information, adjourn the trial either to a fixed date or to a time and place to be determined later. Once the accused has been convicted, however, the powers of the magistrates to adjourn are limited to a period of not more than 3 weeks. Such adjournments may be for example for the purpose of obtaining a medical report or a social inquiry report from a probation officer.

HEARING AT MAGISTRATES' COURT

The hearing of an information or complaint must be in open court. The parties have the right to be represented by counsel or solicitor, and in minor charges the police may conduct the prosecution themselves. If the accused is present and when charged admits the offence, the prosecutor's advocate will state the facts of the case and the accused's advocate will address the court by way of mitigation and the court will proceed to judgment.

In the event of a plea of "not guilty", however, the prosecutor's advocate will open the case and call his witnesses in support, who will be cross-examined by the defendant's advocate. The defendant's advocate will then call his witnesses who will in turn be cross-examined by the prosecutor's advocate.

Normally the defendant's advocate is entitled only to one speech, either before or after calling evidence, except when evidence is given by witnesses for the defendant in addition to the defendant himself and the court agrees. In the event of the defendant's advocate making a second speech in these circumstances, the prosecutor's advocate will also be entitled to a second speech.

The defendant's advocate is entitled when all the evidence has been called for the prosecution, to submit to the court that there is no case to answer. If such a submission is upheld, that is the end of the matter; but if the magistrates consider there is a case to answer, the hearing will proceed as indicated above.

A magistrates' court may either before starting, or at any time during the inquiry, adjourn the hearing, and shall remand the accused (*a*) in custody to be brought before the court at the end of the period of remand, or at such earlier time as the court may require, or (*b*) remand him on bail, that is on his own recognizance with or without sureties. Generally speaking, a magistrates' court may not remand a person for a period exceeding eight clear days.

If, however, the remand is on bail, the court may remand for a longer period provided the accused and the other party (normally the person conducting the prosecution) consent. In the event of illness or accident intervening the above restrictions do not apply.

Magistrates' courts are restricted as to their powers of imposing imprisonment. No imprisonment can be imposed by these courts on any person under 17 years old. They may impose concurrent or consecutive terms of imprisonment subject, however, to certain statutory exceptions, to an aggregate period not to exceed 6 months. When offences triable on indictment are dealt with summarily, the maximum period of consecutive imprisonment is increased to 12 months.

The powers of magistrates as regards imposing prison sentences are further restricted by the provisions of the First Offenders Act, 1958. That Act provided that a magistrates' court shall not pass sentence of imprisonment on a first offender of or over the age of 21 unless the court is of opinion that no other method of dealing with him is appropriate, and must certify accordingly.

A first offender is defined as "a person who has not since attaining the age of 17 been convicted by a court in any part of the United Kingdom of any offence except an offence not punishable with imprisonment".

A summary offence is an offence which, if committed by an adult, is triable by a magistrates' court (apart from statutory exceptions); an indictable offence is one which if committed by an adult, is triable on indictment (apart from certain statutory exceptions) (see section 125 Magistrates' Courts Act, 1952). Persons under 17 years of age are triable by juvenile courts except when the charge is one of homicide.

OFFENCES TRIABLE SUMMARILY OR ON INDICTMENT

Section 18 (1) of the Magistrates' Courts Act, 1952, enacts that an information charging a person who has attained the age of 14 with an offence that is both an indictable offence and a summary offence, shall be dealt with as if the offence were not a summary offence, unless the court having jurisdiction to try the information summarily determines on the application of the prosecutor to do so.

The application must be made before any evidence is called. Subsection (3) of this section empowers the magistrates at any time during the inquiry, subject to certain conditions being satisfied, to proceed to try the case summarily. A similar power in reverse is given by subsection (5) to discontinue a summary trial and proceed to inquire as examining justices.

Section 19 of the Magistrates' Courts Act, 1952, provides that where a person who has attained the age of 17 appears or is brought before a magistrates' court on an information charging him with certain indictable offences which are specified in the first schedule of that Act, and at any time during the inquiry into the offence it appears to the court that their powers of punishment are adequate, and the circumstances do not make the offence one of so serious a character as to warrant trial on indictment, the court may proceed with a view to summary trial. To do this, however, the court shall cause the charge to be written down and read to the accused and inform him of his right to be tried summarily, and if the offence is triable by Quarter Sessions explain to him that in the event of his being convicted he may be committed to Quarter Sessions for sentence.

COMMITTAL TO QUARTER SESSIONS FOR SENTENCE

The limited powers of punishment to which magistrates' courts are restricted have already been mentioned. Sections 28 and 29 of the Magistrates' Courts Act, 1952, however, provide a means by which magistrates, who have dealt with a case by way of summary trial, are empowered to commit convicted persons to Quarter Sessions for sentence. The provisions of section 28, as amended by the Criminal Justice Act, 1961, are to the effect that where a person is convicted by a magistrates' court of an offence punishable on summary conviction with imprisonment, if on the day of such conviction he is not less than 15 but under 21 and the court is of opinion that he should undergo Borstal training, he shall be committed in custody for such purpose; but, as we shall see in Chapter 4, the powers of sentencing by Quarter Sessions are not limited to Borstal training in such cases.

Section 29 provides that when a person not less than 17 years old is convicted on summary trial of an indictable offence triable by Quarter Sessions and the magistrates are of the opinion that greater punishment should be inflicted for the offence than the court has power to inflict, they may similarly commit in custody to Quarter Sessions. (See Chapter 4, p. 93.)

Further reference will be made to these committals in the chapter dealing with trial at Quarter Sessions.

COMMITTAL FOR TRIAL

The third kind of hearing with which magistrates' courts are concerned relates to the proceedings preliminary to trial on indictment. This function can be discharged by a single justice. The evidence of each witness, including the accused if he gives evidence, is taken down by the clerk of the court, read to the witness in the presence of the accused and signed by the witness. Evidence thus obtained becomes a deposition and the witness is then bound over to attend the trial by means of a recognizance which binds him to come to the higher court and give evidence there on pain of paying into the Treasury £x should he fail to turn up when called upon.* This undertaking is set out in a document on the back of which is endorsed the proviso that if the witness attends as required he should be free from all liability.

Provision is also made (see section 5 of the Magistrates' Courts Act, 1952) for the binding over of witnesses to attend the trial conditionally. The purpose of this procedure is to prevent the unnecessary attendance of purely formal witnesses at the trial court. As a safeguard, the section provides means whereby the attendance of such witnesses can be procured, if so desired by either the prosecutor or the person committed for trial.

*See, however, Appendix I, p. 136.

The procedure relating to witnesses will be further referred to in Chapter 4. Since reference is also made in Chapter 2 to the necessary documents that are required on committal of an accused for trial at an Assize or Sessions court, it is not necessary to refer to that aspect in the present chapter.

The committal for trial may, of course, be either in custody or on bail, and the warrant of committal or bail recognizance, as the case may be, shall specify the Assize or Quarter Sessions before which he is to be tried. Where the committal for trial is on bail, the magistrates' clerk shall give notice to the Governor of the prison to which persons are committed by that court in custody, the object of this being, as we will see in a later chapter, to supply the prison Governor with the necessary information on which to compile the calendar for that particular Assize or Quarter Sessions.

VAGRANCY

This is a convenient place in which to refer to a special type of case which comes up for hearing before magistrate's courts, namely charges in connection with vagrancy. There are three main categories of vagrants—idle and disorderly persons, rogues and vagabonds and incorrigible rogues.

Included in the first category are pedlars trading without licence, prostitutes behaving indecently and persons begging alms. All such persons are punishable as idle and disorderly persons by a magistrate's court (see Vagrancy Act, 1824, section 3, and Magistrates' Courts Act, 1952, section 27).

Rogues and vagabonds include not only persons previously convicted as idle and disorderly but also persons who commit a variety of offences as laid down in section 4 of the Vagrancy Act, 1824.

Finally, magistrates are empowered to convict any person as an incorrigible rogue provided that such person has been previously adjudged and convicted as a rogue and vagabond. On conviction they may commit him to prison until the next general or Quarter Sessions of the peace, when he may be further imprisoned for a period not exceeding one year.

JUVENILE COURTS

There is a conclusive presumption that no child under the age of 10 years can be guilty of an offence. Infants between 10 and 14 are presumed not to have sufficient capacity to know that what they did was wrong. This presumption is, however, rebuttable by evidence of design, concealment or exceptional ferocity.

All persons over 14 are presumed to possess a sufficient degree of reason to be responsible for crimes, unless the contrary is proved.

Every juvenile court (outside the Metropolitan Police Court area, which includes the City of London) shall be constituted of not more than three justices from the panel, and shall include a man and a woman.

The main tendency of modern legislation regarding the conduct of proceedings before juvenile courts has been to render them less formal than those of summary courts dealing with offences by adults and at the same time to ensure that such courts are segregated from the other functions of magistrates' courts. With these ends in view, the Children and Young Persons Acts, 1933 to 1963, have laid down certain specific conditions under which juvenile courts shall carry on their work.

No charge against a child or young person shall be heard by a court of summary jurisdiction other than a juvenile court, except when such a person is jointly charged with an adult, or the charge is one of murder or manslaughter.

Juvenile courts shall sit as often as may be necessary. The proceedings shall not take place in a room in which sittings of a court other than a juvenile court are held if a sitting of that other court has been or will be held there within an hour before or after the sitting of the juvenile court.

The form of oath for use in juvenile courts and by children and young persons in other courts, has since 1st February 1964 commenced with the words "I promise before Almighty God' instead of the words "I swear by Almighty God that" (section 28 Children and Young Persons Act, 1963).

Statutory restrictions prevent the attendance at any sitting of a juvenile court of persons other than the following:
   (a) Members and officers of the court.
   (b) Parties to the case before the court, their solicitors and counsel, and witnesses and other persons directly concerned in the case.
   (c) *Bona fide* representatives of newspapers or news agencies.
   (d) Such other persons as the court may specially authorize to be present.

The powers of adjournment of a juvenile court are limited to periods not to exceed 21 days.

Restrictions have also been laid down as to the reporting of proceedings before juvenile courts.

Section 49 of the Children and Young Persons Act, 1933, enacted that no newspaper report of any proceedings in a juvenile court shall reveal the name, address or school, or include any particulars calculated to lead to the identification of any child or young person concerned in those proceedings, either as being the person charged or as being a witness therein. Similar restrictions are placed on the taking of photographs. A proviso to this section, however, gives the court power to dispense with the requirements of the section if satisfied that it is in the interests of justice so to do.

AFFILIATION ORDERS

A summons is issued by way of complaint, which is served on the alleged father of a bastard child (Bastardy Laws Amendment Act, 1872). Section 4 of that Act lays down that a magistrates' court shall hear the evidence of the mother notwithstanding any consent or admission on the part of the defendant.

Magistrates' Courts

The application has generally to be made by a "single" woman within 12 months of the birth of an illegitimate child, unless the alleged father has within the 12 months next after the birth paid money for its maintenance, or at any time within the 12 months next after the man's return to England, on proof that he ceased to reside in England within 12 months next after the birth.

Corroboration in some material particular by evidence other than the mother's is required before a magistrates' court may adjudge a defendant to be the putative father. Such evidence may be in the form of a letter written by the alleged father, or the evidence of an independent witness which supports the mothers claim.

A magistrates' court may order a sum of money, not exceeding 50$s.$ a week, to be paid by the putative father; and where such a periodical order is made the payment is made through the justices' clerk.

The court that makes an affiliation order has power on complaint to revoke, revive or vary the order. It can, for instance, increase or reduce the amount of the weekly payments on evidence being adduced to prove a change of circumstances either way.

An appeal in respect of the making or refusal by the magistrates' court to make such an order lies to Quarter Sessions, and many such appeals occupy the time of Sessions.

DOMESTIC PROCEEDINGS

The expression "domestic proceedings" means proceedings:
(a) Under the Guardianship of Infants Acts, 1886 and 1925.
(b) Under the Summary Jurisdiction (Separation and Maintenance) Acts, 1895 to 1949.
(c) Under section 3 or section 4 of the Maintenance Orders (Facilities for Enforcement) Act, 1920.
(d) Under subsection (3) of section 4 of the Family Allowances Act, 1945, or under that subsection as applied by

subsection (2) of section 19 of the National Insurance Act, 1946.

(*e*) Under section 3 of the Marriage Act, 1949.

The hearing and determination of domestic proceedings are by statute arranged in such manner as may be requisite for separating such hearings from the other business of magistrates' courts. The main purpose of this being so that the proceedings may be conducted with as much priority as possible.

When hearing domestic proceedings, a magistrates' court shall be composed of not more than three justices of the peace, including, so far as practicable, both a man and a woman.

Similar restrictions in line with those already referred to in the earlier paragraphs of this chapter on juvenile courts also apply to domestic courts.

Section 58 of the Magistrates' Courts Act, 1952, lays down restrictions on newspaper reporting of any proceedings before domestic courts. These restrictions, though not quite so stringent as in the case of juvenile courts, restrict the publication of domestic proceedings to the following:

(*a*) The names, addresses and occupation of the parties and witnesses.

(*b*) The grounds of the application.

(*c*) Submissions on points of law and the decision of the court on such submissions.

(*d*) The decision of the court and any observations made by the court in giving it.

One of the important duties of probation officers is, at the request of a domestic court, to attempt to effect a conciliation between the parties. When considering the custody or upbringing of an infant, or the administration of any property is in question, the court shall regard the welfare of the infant as the first and paramount consideration.

The custody of children is one of the main problems which have to be solved by magistrates when they are dealing with domestic proceedings. The guardianship of children becomes of paramount importance, and in matrimonial proceedings a magistrates' court may make an order making provision for the legal custody of any child of the family who is under the age of 16. These powers include, should circumstances justify it, the making of an order for a child to be committed to a specified local authority (Matrimonial Proceedings Act, 1960, section 2).

Magistrates' courts also deal with affiliation, which is the name given to the proceedings brought by the mother in order to compel a man to maintain an illegitimate child of which he is adjudged to be the putative father (Affiliation Proceedings Act, 1957, section 1). Either party, if unsuccessful, that is to say the mother should the magistrates refuse to make an order, or the putative father if the order is made against him, have a right of appeal to Quarter Sessions.

LICENSING

A "justices' licence" means a licence granted by licensing justices under the Licensing Act, 1953. Such licences may be for the sale of intoxicating liquor for consumption either on or off the premises, and are therefore known as a "justices' on-licence" or a "justices' off-licence". Each petty sessional division of a county and each borough having a separate commission of the peace is a licensing district for the purposes of the Licensing Acts.

The duties of licensing justices are discharged by a committee of the justices in and for each licensing district, and are known as the Divisional Licensing Committee or the Borough Licensing Committee, as the case may be. The committee must consist of not less than five justices and not more than fifteen. Licensing justices have a statutory duty to hold a general annual licensing meeting and not less than four nor more than eight transfer sessions in the 12 months beginning with February in every year.

The applicant for a justices' licence shall, if so required by the licensing justices, attend in person, except in the case of an application for renewal, when he will not be required to attend unless objection is made to the renewal.

When hearing an application for the grant of a new licence, the justices have an absolute discretion either to grant or refuse the application, subject to appeal to Quarter Sessions. The justices may also attach to the grant of a new justices' on-licence such conditions governing tenure and other matters as they think proper in the interests of the public. A provisional licence may be granted, subject to its being declared final on proof that certain conditions have been complied with.

Another kind of licence which comes up for consideration by licensing justices is a transfer licence. In effect this amounts to substituting another person for the present holder of the licence. Such a licence shall not be granted except in the circumstances as set out in section 7 of the Licensing Act, 1964, i.e. where the holder has died, become incapable through illness, is adjudged bankrupt, gives up occupation of the premises, or if the occupier is about to quit the premises and wilfully fails to apply for a renewal of the licence or where the owner of the premises has been granted a protection order.

Occasional licences have also to be applied for. These are, in effect, applications for an extension of the normal licensing hours in relation to some special event such as a wedding reception, dance, dinner or some special occasion such as New Year's Eve. Such a licence, of course, applies only to the day in question for which it is applied for.

The powers of licensing justices to refuse the renewal or transfer of old on-licences are limited by section 12 of the Licensing Act, 1964, subsections (3) and (4), and amount in the case of old beerhouses to failure to produce evidence of good character, disorderly character of the premises or if the applicant has been previously disqualified.

Other than old beerhouses, the only grounds for refusal are that the applicant is not a fit and proper person or that the licensed premises have been ill-conducted.

Section 12 of the Licensing Act, 1961, provided that no justices' licences granted after the coming into force of this section (the first of November 1961) shall require confirmation.

In the event of licensing justices being of the opinion that the question of the renewal of an old on-licence requires consideration they shall refer the matter to the compensation authority (see Chapter 4) which is a committee of Quarter Sessions. The majority of such references relate to "old beerhouse licences" and of recent years have become increasingly rare.

Another form of application is for the removal of a justices' licence from the premises for which it was granted to another premises. Such removals may be ordinary or special.

BOOKMAKER'S PERMIT AND BETTING OFFICE LICENCE

Section 2 of the Betting, Gaming and Lotteries Act, 1963, enacts that no person shall act as a bookmaker on his own account unless he is the holder of a "bookmaker's permit". This Act also makes provision for the licensing of betting offices.

The authority responsible for the grant of bookmakers' permits, betting agency permits and betting office licences shall be known as the "appropriate authority", and in any petty sessional area in England consists of a committee constituted in the prescribed manner of not less than 5 nor more than 15 of the justices acting for that area; the quorum being three. The clerk to the justices is the clerk to the appropriate authority.

Each appropriate authority shall for each year fix four days in compliance with the terms set out in the statute, as days on which they will hold meetings for considering any applications for a bookmaker's permit, betting agency permit or betting office licence then awaiting consideration.

The grounds on which such applications can be refused are laid down in the 1963 Act, and consist in the case of applications for the grant or renewal of a bookmaker's permit (*a*) if the appropriate authority are not satisfied that the applicant is a fit and proper person to be the holder of a bookmaker's permit, or (*b*) the authority are satisfied that, if the permit were to be granted or renewed, the business to which it relates would be managed by, or carried on for the benefit of, a person other than the applicant, being a person who would himself be refused the grant or renewal.

Whilst the grounds on which an application for the grant or renewal of a betting office licence can be referred are that the authority are not satisfied (*a*) that the premises are or will be enclosed; that there are or will be means of access between the premises and a street otherwise than through other premises used for the effecting with persons resorting to those other premises of transactions other than betting transactions; (*b*) that the premises are not suitable for use as a licensed betting office; or that the grant or renewal would be inexpedient having regard to the demand for the time being in the locality for the facilities afforded by licensed betting offices and to the number of such offices for the time being available to meet that demand; or that the premises have not been properly conducted under the licence. There is a right of appeal to Quarter Sessions against the refusal of an appropriate authority to grant or renew a bookmaker's permit, betting agency permit or betting office licence. This factor will be dealt with in Chapter 4.

CIVIL DEBTS

Proceedings for the recovery of certain civil debts are begun by a complaint, which is made where the person in regard to whom it is made is liable to have an order made upon him either to pay money or to do an act which, contrary to law, he has refused or neglected to do.

A magistrates' court has power to make an order on complaint for payment of any money recoverable summarily as a civil debt. In proceedings for the recovery or enforcement of a sum so recoverable the court has no power to issue a warrant for the arrest of a defendant who does not appear. This restriction also applies to bastardy complaints; whereas in criminal matters a magistrates' court has power to compel the attendance of a defendant in order to answer a charge.

An order for the payment of a civil debt may be enforced by the issue of a distress warrant or by a warrant of commitment only when the defendant has been served with a copy of the order (if not made in his presence). The court must, however, be satisfied as to the defendant's means before issuing a committal warrant, a further necessary preliminary being the issue and service of a judgment summons on the defendant.

Though but brief reference has of necessity been made to the work of magistrates' courts with regard to the collection and administration of monies, these duties have of recent years increased enormously, and in most magistrates' courts these duties alone occupy the full-time services of several members of the staff of the clerk to the justices.

It is now proposed to pass from the actual activities of magistrates' courts to the transition stage which will in due course lead to a survey of the work of Quarter Sessions and Assizes.

CHAPTER 2

Transition from Magistrates' Courts to Quarter Sessions and Assize Courts

Committal for trial — Depositions — Committals for sentence — Indictments — *Nolle prosequi* — Fixing of dates — Arrangement of lists — Appeals — Calendars — County day agenda

COMMITTAL FOR TRIAL

OF THE three main categories with which we have seen that magistrates' courts are concerned, it is mainly the preliminary hearings to determine whether there is a prima facie case on which to commit a defendant to an Assize court or Quarter Sessions for trial by jury that we will be concerned with in this chapter, together with the procedure relative to convicted persons who are committed to Quarter Sessions for sentence.

Due notice having been given, defendants are normally committed for trial, or for sentence to Quarter Sessions under the provisions of section 9 (1) (*a*) of the Magistrates' Courts Act, 1952, or the provisions of sections 28 or 29 of that Act, respectively, the committal being to the next available sitting of the appropriate Quarter Sessions. There is, however, one important exception to this general rule. Section 10 (2) of the Magistrates' Courts Act, 1952, has enacted that where a person is to be committed for trial on bail to a court of Quarter Sessions, and that session is due to be held within 5 days from the date of committal, then the petty sessional court may commit him to the next session but one.

In actual practice this power has proved to be most useful,

since it prevents a certain number of late committals, which invariably lead to complications and delay. It also has the more practical result of deferring a hearing, which in all probability would in any event be unlikely to take place before the later date.

DEPOSITIONS

When committing a case for trial either to Assizes or Quarter Sessions, the clerk to the justices must take care to ensure that all the requisite documents that will be required for the trial are made available to the trial court. The original depositions, which will have been taken down either in longhand or by means of a silent typewriter, are the first consideration. The clerk to the justices must see that each deposition is read to the witness after he has given his evidence and also that the witness has signed the deposition. Each witness has to enter into a recognizance to attend the trial court and give evidence.* A further necessity with regard to the depositions of witnesses who have given evidence at the magistrates' court is to make sure that one of the magistrates have certified that the depositions are in order, and generally to ascertain that the various requirements relating to depositions have been carried out.

A form also has to be sent with each case setting out the names of any witnesses who have been conditionally bound over to attend the trial (the importance of this will appear in Chapter 4). Even if no witnesses are in fact so bound over, the Court of Criminal Appeal has decreed that a nil return showing that no witnesses have been so bound over should be sent to the trial court. If the defendant has been committed for trial on bail, the bail form should be sent to the Assize or Sessions court and the proper officer of the court will attach it to the indictment when it is drawn.

The clerk to the justices must also forward a list of exhibits together with such original exhibits as have been produced to

*See Appendix I, p. 136.

the court during the course of the preliminary hearing. These exhibits usually consist of written statements made by the accused — and these should be attached to the depositions. The usual procedure is for the police to retain any exhibits of a bulky or heavy description, whilst documentary matters such as letters, pawn tickets, consignment notes, etc., are retained by the court.

It is also of assistance if the names of solicitors and counsel both for the prosecution and for the defence, if known to the justices' clerk, are forwarded, together with the name of the officer in charge of the case. A final matter to be checked is whether the charge or charges on which the defendant or defendants appeared before the magistrates are in fact the same as those on which they are committed for trial.

The clerk to the justices having carried out his duties, the clerk of the assize or the clerk of the peace, as the case may be, takes over in order to prepare for the day of trial. The first thing that he must do on receipt of the committal papers is to satisfy himself that all the above matters have in fact been dealt with by the clerk to the justices, the next sequence of events being to have copies made of the original depositions and exhibits. This should be done as speedily as possible so that copies are readily available for the defence when asked for, and as clerks to justices in many cases type original depositions, the introduction of copying machines has made the copying of these documents infinitely quicker and easier. In the era before machines came into use, all depositions were in manuscript and often very difficult to decipher, and the copying had to be done by typists and every single word checked. When one looks back now, it is hard to understand how this part of the work was ever kept up to date. No longer can counsel refer to typists' errors — errors, if any there are, were perpetrated during the original hearing before the magistrates, and the machine has dutifully reproduced what was recorded on that occasion.

In order to satisfy the requirements of the court, it is the usual practice to have not less than eight or nine copies of the depositions run off. In cases where several defendants are involved and are represented by separate solicitors and counsel, it is necessary to have even more copies available.

Appeals from magistrates' courts to Quarter Sessions will be referred to later in this chapter. In the event, however, of a person convicted in a magistrates' court wanting to appeal on a point of law, he must do so by way of case stated to the Divisional Court of the High Court of Justice; in which event he will not be able to exercise his right of appeal to Quarter Sessions. The clerk to the justices will then have to draw up the case for presentation to the High Court on behalf of his justices.

COMMITTALS FOR SENTENCE

In addition to cases committed for trial, Quarter Sessions now deal with what are known as committals for sentence, reference to which has already been made in Chapter 1. When the Criminal Justice Act, 1948, came into force, all Sessions, other than London, had to deal with these committals for sentence through the Appeal Committee of Quarter Sessions. Quite apart from the fact that this resulted in a considerable interference with the normal appeals which also had to be heard, there were other difficulties of administration which resulted. When, therefore, the Criminal Justice Act, 1962, finally abolished the distinction between Quarter Sessions and the Appeal Committee as from June 1962, the innovation was very welcome to Quarter Sessions. Particularly is this so in view of the fact that the recent extension in jurisdiction which was given to petty sessional courts at the same time has resulted, as was anticipated, in a material increase in the number of persons who are committed to Sessions for sentence.

Accordingly, section 28 of the Magistrates' Courts Act, 1952, as amended by the Criminal Justice Act, 1961, in conjunction with section 20 of the Criminal Justice Act, 1948, makes provision for persons over the age of 15 and under 21 who are convicted at a magistrates' court of any offence which is punishable in the case of an adult with imprisonment to be committed under the provisions of section 28 with a view to being sent to Borstal training. In these cases Sessions may sentence to Borstal training or deal with the offender in any manner in which the magistrates' court might have dealt with him. Under section 20 (5) (d) of the Criminal Justice Act, 1948, the defendant may appeal to the Court of Criminal Appeal against the sentence of Quarter Sessions only if he is sentenced to Borstal training.

Section 19 of the Magistrates' Courts Act, 1952, gives power to a magistrates' court to deal summarily with certain indictable cases which otherwise would only be triable on indictment.

Section 29 of the Magistrates' Courts Act, 1952, in conjunction with section 29 of the Criminal Justice Act, 1948, makes provision for persons of not less than 17 years of age who are convicted at a magistrates' court on a summary trial, of an indictable offence (under subsection (3) of section 18 or under section 19 of the Magistrates' Courts Act, 1952) to be committed for sentence if the magistrates' court is of opinion, having regard to the character and antecedents of the prisoner, that a greater punishment should be inflicted than such court has the power to inflict. A defendant may appeal to the Court of Criminal Appeal against the sentence only if Sessions passes a greater sentence than the magistrates' court could have passed. Should, however, Quarter Sessions deal with a defendant under the provisions of section 20 (5) (a) (ii) of the Criminal Justice Act, 1948, i.e. "In any manner in which the court of summary jurisdiction might have dealt with him" such as, for instance, by putting him on probation or conditionally discharging him, there is no right of appeal against such a sentence.

If the accused person pleaded guilty at the hearing before the magistrates, there is no reason, apart from medical evidence or some vital report not yet being available, why the accused should not be dealt with as speedily as possible. The plea of guilty before the justices must, however, have been a clear and unambiguous one; if not, it should be treated as if the defendant had in fact pleaded not guilty and he should be tried accordingly, in which case the statutory period of 14 days during which a notice of appeal against his conviction at the magistrates' court can be entered by the accused, must be allowed to elapse before he is brought before the Sessions. If, however, he appeals to Quarter Sessions against his conviction by the magistrates' court, the appeal must be heard and dismissed before he can be sentenced.

Should the police desire to serve notices under the provisions of section 23 of the Criminal Justice Act, 1948, at least three clear days will have to elapse after the service of the notices before the accused can be dealt with by Sessions, otherwise the notices will be invalid and the court will be unable to sentence him to corrective training or preventive detention.

From the above it is at once apparent what confusion could arise should Quarter Sessions inadvertently deal with a person who pleaded not guilty before the magistrates prior to the elapse of the statutory period during which an appeal against such a conviction may be brought. It is the practice for defendants to be committed to a specific sitting of Quarter Sessions; thus the intake of fresh cases during the early stages of a current session present no problems, since there is plenty of time for the 14 days to elapse before the commencing date of the session to which the defendant has been committed. A more watchful eye must of necessity be kept on committals once a clear period of 14 days no longer exists prior to the opening day of the next session.

It quite frequently happens that an appeal is in fact entered against the conviction before the magistrates. Once the notice of appeal is received, the clerk of the peace has to enter the appeal for hearing at the next practicable date of the court sitting for appeals. Busy Quarter Sessions fix annually the dates on which appeals will be heard. The chairman of quarter sessions can, should the state of the appeal list warrant it, fix additional dates for these hearings. The abolition of the Appeal Committee has made this easier than formerly. If Quarter Sessions after hearing an appeal against conviction by a defendant who has been committed to them for sentence, dismiss the appeal, they can only proceed to sentence the defendant if he was in fact committed to the current session. If this is not so, he will have to be put back in custody to be dealt with at the next session, when doubtless it will be arranged for him to make an early appearance.

INDICTMENTS

The next consideration is to get the indictment settled. This is a document setting out the charges. The great majority of indictments are settled by the clerk of assize or the clerk of the peace. The ordinary run-of-the-mill cases such as burglary, shopbreaking, housebreaking, larceny, possessing housebreaking implements by night, receiving stolen property, driving under the influence of drink, etc., normally present no special difficulties; and it is only in the more complicated cases or where special difficulty arises that the indictment is settled by counsel. It has to be remembered, however, that the prosecution are always entitled to require that an indictment should be settled by counsel; and the clerk of assize or the clerk of the peace can likewise require counsel to do so if he thinks fit. The usual practice is that such cases as false pretences, involved cases of receiving, embezzlement and, indeed, any committal where possible alternative charges may be laid, are invariably settled by counsel. In the case of prosecutions by Government Departments, e.g. Revenue or Post Office, the solicitor to the department usually assumes responsibility for having the indictment settled.

Since the Indictments Act, 1915, most of the technicalities in connection with indictments have disappeared. The Court of Criminal Appeal has on several occasions commented adversely on unnecessarily long indictments.

The complexity of the indictment varies from case to case. On the one hand one has the simple case of a single defendant charged with a single offence; on the other hand, a case involving a number of defendants who are charged with a whole series of offences of a similar nature. As already indicated, the majority of the straightforward cases present no real difficulty. But in settling the simplest and most elementary indictments it is necessary to be thoroughly conversant with the full facts as set out in the depositions. To take a simple example, before settling an indictment charging a defendant with being in unlawful possession of housebreaking implements by night, it is necessary to make sure that the evidence as disclosed on the depositions satisfies the ingredients of the alleged offence — in this instance the alleged offence must appear from the depositions to have taken place during the statutory legal definition of night, i.e. between 9 p.m. and 6 a.m. the following morning.

Though I have referred to certain charges as "run-of-the-mill" cases, it by no means follows that such cases present no difficulty regarding the settling of indictments. Five or six defendants may be jointly committed for trial on a variety of charges. The result may well be an indictment containing several counts, some of which relate to certain of the defendants and other counts to other various combinations of the defendants. Great care has to be taken to ensure that the property relating to each charge is properly described in the material count of the indictment.

Further, the clerk of the assize or the clerk of the peace has a duty to see that either a copy of the full indictment or an accurate abstract is placed before the judge or chairman. The normal practice is to have accurate abstracts prepared. Indeed, it is these abstracts that serve the basis of arraigning a defendant. Great care must be taken, therefore, to see that such requirements as, for example, "with intent to deceive" or other similar essentials are included in the abstract. In the case of a charge of false pretences, the full false pretence has to be included in the abstract, as the defendant is entitled to know exactly what the charge against him is.

It sometimes happens that when an indictment has to be settled, it is evident from the evidence contained in the depositions that a charge additional to the one on which the defendant has been committed for trial can properly be added to the indictment. An instance that comes readily to mind is where, on a defendant being arrested, an assault takes place on a police officer, who as a result suffers bodily injury. Here in addition to the count charging the accused with the offence for which he was arrested, a count is added in the indictment to cover the assault. In such cases, that is, where counts differ materially from or are additional to the charge or charges on which the defendant has been committed for trial, the clerk of the assize or the clerk of the peace has a duty to notify the prosecution and the prisoner of the facts — and if the indictment be settled by counsel for the prosecution, notify the prisoner as soon as possible.

Rule 13 of the Indictments Rules, made under the Indictments Act, 1915, and the Administration of Justice (Miscellaneous Provisions) Act, 1933, places a duty on the officer in charge of indictments, after a bill of indictment has been drawn up and signed by the clerk, to supply the accused person, on request, with a copy of the indictment free of charge. The purpose of this being to ensure that the accused person is fully aware of the charges which he has to meet.

The indictment having been settled, it is then formally preferred, and, subject to his being satisfied that the provisions of section 2 (2) of the Administration of Justice (Miscellaneous Provisions) Act, 1933, have been carried out, the proper officer of the court then signs the bill of indictment and it thereupon becomes an indictment, and from then onwards can be quashed or amended only by order of the court. Section 2 (2) referred to above reads as follows: "A person may be proceeded against, indicted, tried and punished for an offence in any county or place in England in which he is apprehended or is in custody, as if the offence had been committed in that county or place."

The proper officer of the court ought not to sign a bill of indictment, whether drawn in his office or by counsel, unless he is satisfied that it is correctly drawn. In any case in which he feels himself unable so to sign, the judge of Assize or the chairman of quarter sessions is the final arbiter. The proviso to section 2 (1) of the Administration of Justice (Miscellaneous Provisions) Act, 1933, enacts that if the judge or chairman of the court is satisfied that the requirements have been complied with, he may, on the application of the prosecution or of his own motion, direct the proper officer to sign the indictment.

One further point remains to be mentioned regarding indictments, and that is that no indictment can be preferred at any Assizes or Quarter Sessions after the first working day of those Assizes or Sessions without leave of the judge or chairman. Reference will be made to this procedure in Chapter 4.

The indictment settled, copies of the original depositions made, together with copies of any exhibits that have been forwarded from the magistrates' court, such as written statements of the accused, lists of missing property, etc., the clerk of the assize or the clerk of the peace will then distribute copies as requested to defending solicitors, the prosecuting solicitor or the defendant himself. For these copies he is entitled to charge the prosecution the sum of 4*d.* a folio (72 words) and the defence 1½*d.* a folio.*

NOLLE PROSEQUI (PROSECUTE NO FURTHER)

Proceedings upon an indictment pending in any court may be stayed by the entry of a *nolle prosequi* at any time after the indictment is signed and before judgment. This can only be done on the direction of the Attorney-General. Either the prosecutor or the accused person can apply to the Attorney-General for his direction.

*These charges are no longer enforced by courts within the Greater London Area.

Such application is usually directed owing to the physical or mental incapacity of the accused person, and runs as follows:

The Queen v. *A.B.*

Let a *nolle prosequi* be entered in my name in the case of the above-named, whose trial at the . . . Assizes (or Quarter Sessions) in a charge of . . . now stands adjourned, in order to discharge all the further proceedings therein AND for so doing this shall be your warrant.

....
Her Majesty's Attorney-General.

C.D.
Clerk of Assize.

FIXING OF DATES

Courts of assize, oyer and terminer, and gaol delivery, including the Central Criminal Court and the two Crown courts, are now part of the High Court, and their records are those of that Court.

Courts acting under a Commission of Assize try only such criminal offences as are sent to them for trial, whereas the ordinary circuit courts of oyer and terminer, and gaol delivery have jurisdiction to try any offence triable at common law or by statute in the district for which they are commissioned.

The sittings of courts of Assize are regulated by Orders in Council (see section 72 of the Supreme Court of Judicature (Consolidation) Act, 1925). It is by virtue of this section that the Crown may from time to time, by Order in Council, make orders for the regulation of circuits. Assizes have to be held at least twice in every year.

The Central Criminal Court used to have to hold sessions at least twelve times a year; since 1965, however, the sessions have been reduced to four but this is a technical change which does not affect the business of the courts at the Old Bailey. The Lord Chief Justice fixes and causes to be published the date of the beginning of each session of the Central Criminal Court (see Schedule 1, Administration of Justice Act, 1964).

A court of Assize may be held in any building, but it must

be in a place not more than 3 miles distant from the area of jurisdiction for which the court is held.

The dates for holding Quarter and Intermediate Sessions are fixed annually at the Michaelmas Quarter Sessions. The date of each Quarter Sessions, namely Michaelmas, Epiphany, Easter and Midsummer, were up to the 30th April 1962 regulated by statute and had to be held within the period of 21 days immediately preceding or immediately following the four calendar quarter days, i.e. the 29th September, the 25th December, the 25th March and the 24th June. Section 4 (1) of the Criminal Justice Act, 1962, which came into operation on the 30th April 1962, however, enacted that courts of Quarter Sessions (other than London) "shall be held at such times as the justices for that county or borough think fit . . . but shall be held at least four times a year". The first day of each Quarter Sessions is known as the County Day. A duty is laid on the clerk of the peace to lay before the court for approval at the Michaelmas Sessions a list of the days for holding Sessions in the ensuing year. It is also the practice at the same time in busy Sessions to approve a similar list of dates for the hearing of appeals. Once fixed, the four Quarter Sessions dates cannot be altered except by the approval of the court of Quarter Sessions. The Intermediate Sessions can, however, be cancelled by the chairman, should the amount of work justify such action on his part. Of recent years such a situation has seldom arisen.

Once the dates are approved by the court, the clerk of the peace has to circulate them to all the clerks to the justices who sit in the various petty sessional divisions of the county from which defendants are committed for trial to the Sessions. He also has to send copies of these dates to the police, the sheriff and the governors of the prisons. It is of the utmost importance that these dates should be known as soon as possible, since the committal for trial at Sessions has to be to a definite session, and to the earliest one possible. Since the 1st April 1965, when the Administration of Justice Act, 1964, came into operation, county days in the five Quarter Sessions areas which are included in Greater London are no longer required. The fixation of Quarter Sessions in these areas being now administered by the Administrative Committee of Quarter Sessions in each area. The Committee being composed of the chairman and justices in each area.

ARRANGEMENT OF LISTS

It has to be remembered that whereas the type of case which is committed for trial to Assizes may well occupy the judge for several days or even weeks, those that are committed to Sessions are often disposed of within a day, and it is the exception rather than the rule for cases to occupy Quarter Sessions for more than 2-3 days. Having regard to this factor, therefore, it follows that the points to which I am about to refer in the ensuing paragraphs apply of necessity primarily to Quarter Sessions, though the one great uncertainty — the time that any case will take to hear — makes the fixing of hearing dates in advance, whether at Assizes or Quarter Sessions, subject to a certain degree of chance.

The next duty to be performed at the committal court will be for the appropriate official to go through all the depositions and papers relating to committal cases with a view to ascertaining whether each case is likely to result in a plea of guilty or of not guilty.

When the date of the next Assize or Session is about 10 days off, it will be necessary to consider the position regarding jurors (this aspect will be fully dealt with in Chapter 3). For the moment all that need be said is that due thought has to be given to the question when the services of jurors are likely to be required; and with this end in view the clerk of assize or the clerk of the peace must make sure that the precepts signed by the judge, or in the case of Sessions by two magistrates, is sent to the sheriff, so that he receives in reasonable time notice to provide a panel of jurors.

There is, of course, no set system for sorting out cases at the pre-trial stage. It may, however, be found convenient to segregate them into four main groups — certain pleas of guilty, certain pleas of not guilty, possible pleas of guilty — where it is worth taking a chance at listing the case without witnesses—and finally probable fights, where the odds are in favour of a fight, and it is therefore desirable to have the witnesses in attendance.

It is usually possible, in view of the inflated size of calendars, so to arrange the list, at any rate in so far as Sessions are concerned, that only pleas of guilty and committals for sentence, together with applications for the restoration of driving licences, breaches of requirements by persons on probation and conditional discharges, and any judgments respited from the previous Sessions are dealt with in the early days of a new session. Such an arrangement, if possible — although, of course, each clerk in charge of the list will have his own course of action dictated for him by such factors as the number of courts available for hearing cases and the number of likely pleas of guilty and whether the accused has been committed in custody or on bail — will result not only in the saving of time and inconvenience to both jurors and witnesses, but also in a material saving of costs to the ratepayers. The more cases that can be marked "no witnesses", the better. Having regard to the more serious nature of cases that are committed to Assizes, the clerk of assize obviously has greater problems in arranging his list of cases for hearing.

No one, of course, can guarantee, even where all the witnesses in a case have been conditionally bound over and the accused has made a written statement admitting his guilt, that on his appearance in the dock at the trial court he will not change his mind and plead not guilty. It quite frequently happens nowadays that written statements of confession are challenged on the ground that they have not been obtained voluntarily. In that event the case has to be put back for hearing on a later date in the assize or session, but in the majority of such cases the plea of guilty is maintained and the case can, therefore, be disposed of with the minimum of inconvenience and delay.

The making up of a list for the hearing of cases at Assizes or Quarter Sessions cannot, of course, be left until the last moment. Many people are interested in knowing as soon as possible when any particular case is likely to come up for hearing. The police require reasonable time in which to notify witnesses, a process which is usually done through the medium of the officer in charge of the case in question. Timely warning must also be given to probation officers so that they can have their reports ready for the court. Then there are the parents and other interested persons who may desire to give evidence on behalf of the accused persons. In the London area it is possible by co-operation with the officers responsible for compiling the lists at the Central Criminal Court, Inner London Sessions and Middlesex Area Sessions for a barrister who happens to be briefed in several cases listed on the same day at these three courts to put in an appearance on behalf of his clients at each of them.

Various factors which can be taken into account when compiling a list of cases for hearing include the following. The judge or chairman, as the case may be, will vary as regards the speed with which he completes his work. Even then pleas of guilty vary enormously. The case of an undefended prisoner on his own, charged with a single offence (even assuming that he asks for a dock brief), may require a comparatively short time to be completed, whilst an indictment which contains several counts and charges four or five defendants, who are separately represented by counsel, may take up very much more time than could have been foreseen. Committals for sentence, whilst normally not occupying a great deal of time, are still inclined to take longer rather than shorter time than expected. This is especially the case in regard to juvenile delinquents; often, in addition to probation officers' reports, there are also reports from approved schools and other school reports to be considered. Very often, too, in these cases the parents desire to give evidence on behalf of their sons or daughters, as the case may be.

When compiling the lists for a new session and allocating the chosen cases to such courts as are available, more often than not the clerk has no knowledge regarding representation on behalf of the defence. There is always the possibility, too, that the accused will wait until his appearance in court before applying for legal aid, in which event, if the case is of any great complexity, some delay is inevitable and should it transpire that witnesses are vital for the defence it may even result in an adjournment of the hearing to a day later in the assize or session. Whilst judges and chairmen vary in the speed with which they complete their work, the same observation not unnaturally applies also to counsel. At Assizes and the Central Criminal Court the most serious cases are allocated to the judge in commission on that particular circuit. At the latter court murder trials and suchlike cases being heard by the High Court judge whose duty it is to attend that particular session. In a similar way it is usual to allocate the more complicated or serious cases to the chairman of quarter sessions.

Even if it should prove impossible to complete the hearing of all the cases that have been set down for hearing on any particular day, it is desirable, if at all possible, to take all the pleas; this enables any prisoner who so desires to apply for a dock brief or legal aid, and also clears the air with regard to the possibility of any case turning out to be an unexpected trial. Where possible, the taking of the pleas in all cases prior to the midday adjournment of the court, has obvious advantages as regards the effective compilation of the list for the next day's work. The sooner that the list is compiled, the better. It has, however, to be borne in mind that at the midday adjournment there is always the unknown factor of what will happen during the afternoon sitting to be taken into account, and this fact alone is sufficient to make it desirable for the list to be drawn up on a provisional basis, subject to confirmation on the rising of the court.

So much for pleas of guilty, etc.; it is the pleas of not guilty, however, which give the real headaches to those in charge of the lists. It is usually possible to obtain much useful and helpful information from defending solicitors and barristers' clerks. Many unknown factors, however, tend to make the accurate forecasting of the probable length of any contested case of substance extremely hazardous. On the one hand, it is the duty of all those responsible for compiling court lists to help both sides whenever possible by fixing a date for hearing. It is seldom possible in practice to do this without the accompanying warning that the fixture must be subject to a "part heard". It is in fact the part heard case that has overrun its allotted time that is the real bugbear; it may well result in displacing the next case for hearing from its fixed date, by which time the date has arrived for the next fixture. This problem is, of course, much more serious at Assizes than at Sessions, because a judge going on circuit has a time limit fixed for his sitting at any assize town in that circuit, and if he does not exhaust his list by the time his sitting at the next assize town is due the remaining cases have to be transferred to that town. To avert such a disorganization it is now the practice to assign long cases to a special commissioner.

The larger the number of courts which a clerk has available for hearing cases, the easier it is to ensure against unexpected delays, since it is always possible to include a "float" of cases which are available for transference from one court to another to fill any unexpected gap. Where, however, the clerk has only one or two courts available, a certain wastage of court time is almost unavoidable; on the whole, this may well be more desirable than the alternative of overloading a list and putting a large number of witnesses, jurors, counsel, etc., to what may well turn out to be unnecessary inconvenience.

APPEALS

Whilst considering the allocation of work, it may not be out of place to say a few words here with regard to the hearing of appeals from magistrates' courts by Quarter Sessions. So much time is required nowadays for dealing with crime at those courts that the time which of necessity has to be taken up for the hearing of appeals is somewhat grudgingly spared. The first point to bear in mind regarding appeals is that the clerk of the peace has a statutory duty to notify both the appellant and the respondent of the date on which an appeal will be heard by Quarter Sessions. In the case of appeals against refusals by licensing committees to grant either bookmakers' permits or betting office licences there is a statutory obligation to give at least seven clear days' notice. The normal practice is to give this amount of notice to all appellants wherever possible. The arranging of a list for the hearing of appeals is in many ways fraught with more uncertainty than is the case with trials by jury. An appellant has a statutory right to abandon an appeal at any time before the hearing, and provided that he does so three clear days before the date fixed for the hearing, he cannot be mulcted in costs.

Another factor that makes for uncertainty is that, whilst appellants who have been convicted of motoring offences enter appeals against both conviction and sentence, it quite often happens that the appeal against conviction is abandoned in court or the appeal against sentence becomes one only against the imposition of a period of disqualification.

CALENDARS

The compilation of the calendar, which includes the particulars relating to the accused persons who are awaiting trial at Assizes or Sessions, is a matter for the prison governor to arrange. He compiles the calendar from the bail certificates which he receives from the various magistrates' courts in the county; the governors of remand homes also supply particulars of any persons who are in their custody awaiting trial. Those persons who are committed to the prison governor in custody, are, of course, already known to him. Out of these components the calendar is duly comprised and a number is allotted to each person who is committed for trial. These numbers are retained by the accused throughout the session. It should be added that it is the duty of the clerk of assize or the clerk of the peace to inform the prison governor as soon as possible of any cases which have to be carried over to the next session; this is not always easy to do until the next session is only a few days off, since once a case has been notified to the prison governor as having been sent over it cannot be dealt with until that session has commenced. At Assizes it may be possible to transfer cases not reached to the next town for hearing cases on that circuit.

An advance copy of the calendar is sent to Assizes or Sessions on the day preceding the first working day of a new Assizes or Sessions. At Assizes this is known as Commission Day. This advance copy is of necessity not complete; so it is followed by a later edition, which may not be available until some time during the first working day. Even this copy may not be complete owing to the arrival of late committals. A practice has been adopted of recent years whereby separate sheets containing the particulars of these late editions to the calendar are printed, so that they can be sent to the courts concerned and attached as appendices to the main calendar.

The prison governor also supplies Assize and Sessions courts with a full list of the previous convictions of all the persons who appear in the calendar so far as he has been able to ascertain them. In the event of any medical reports being available, these are also sent for the assistance of the court. Where available, though this is no longer a matter of compulsion, any reports as to the suitability for Borstal training, detention centre training, corrective training or preventive detention are also forwarded for the court's information.

The indictments having been drawn up and signed, depositions and exhibits copied, the lists made up, the calendar and other antecedent information all made available and due notice having been given to ensure that all the different persons concerned in the business of the court are warned to attend, all is now set for the trial by jury to commence. Before dealing with this all-important aspect of the superior courts, it is proposed to deal with the very human subject of jurors, which, after all is said and done, is the main reason why many defendants elect to be tried at Quarter Sessions. To this end I propose to devote the next chapter to the subject of jurors, and in Chapter 4 to deal with trial by jury.

COUNTY DAY AGENDA

Before, however, finally leaving the transition stage, in order to complete the picture, it is necessary to refer to certain duties which fall to the clerks of the peace in relation to the four county days of a Quarter Sessions.

The clerk of the peace is responsible for drawing up the agenda for each county day. The conduct of business at Quarter Sessions is regulated by Standing Orders which are approved by the court of Quarter Sessions and cannot be altered or revoked without due notice, and then only by the approval of Quarter Sessions itself. This applies to the conduct of criminal work and to the hearing of appeals from the magistrates' courts by Sessions. Rules for the conduct of licensing work at Sessions are also made by the court, but they are subject to the approval of the Secretary of State.

Certain items, such as the minutes of the last quarter day to be read, are always on the agenda; the usual practice nowadays is that the minutes are circulated, and unless any justice wants to raise any point, this item is generally a formality and the chairman signs them forthwith. There is also invariably an item to cover the bringing to the notice of the court of any statutes, parliamentary bills and other proceedings that are destined to affect the work of Quarter Sessions. It quite often happens that there are in fact no such matters to be brought to the notice of the court.

Other items that have to be included are: at the Michaelmas

Quarter Session the appointment of Assessors under the Clergy Discipline Act, 1892 (Trienally), and it is at these Sessions that the clerk of the peace lays before the court for their approval a list of the days for holding the several sessions and appeal sittings in the ensuing year.

At the Epiphany Quarter Session the report of the County Compensation Committee has to be considered, and the County Compensation Committee have to be appointed. Further, at this session the members of the Visiting Committees are appointed in accordance with the Prison Rules, 1949, made by the Secretary of State by virtue of the powers given to him in section 53 of the Criminal Justice Act, 1948, for the various prisons to which persons may be committed by the particular court of Quarter Sessions. The justices so appointed are known as prison visitors. The Secretary of State also appoints boards of visitors for every remand home, detention centre and Borstal institution.

At the Easter Quarter Sessions the justices who are to represent the court on the Standing Joint Committee are appointed, the practice being for them to be nominated by their respective petty sessional benches.

Finally, on this aspect of his duties, the clerk of the peace has to enter the minutes of the proceedings of the court in a book to be kept for that purpose. As already stated, these various duties, since the 1st April 1965, have to be dealt with by the new Quarter Sessions Committees in the Greater London Area.

CHAPTER 3

Jurors

Precept — Jury panel — Jury excuses — Empanelling juries — Penalty for non-appearance — Challenge to jurors — Putting in charge — Considering verdict — Cummunications to judge or chairman — Taking of verdict — Payment of jurors

THE main distinction between trials before magistrates and trials at Assizes or Quarter Sessions, is that, whilst the former are often referred to as summary justice, the latter are familiarly known as trial by jury.

Trial by jury was introduced long before many of the present courts of Quarter Sessions were brought into being. Section 20 of the Juries Act, 1825, provides that the Court of Queen's Bench, and all courts of oyer and terminer, gaol delivery . . . (and) sessions of the peace in England and Wales shall respectively have and exercise the same power and authority as they have heretofore had and exercised in issuing any writ or precept . . . for the return of a jury for the trial of any issue before any of such courts respectively, or for the amending or enlarging the panel of jurors returned for the trial of any such issue; and the return to every such writ, precept, award or order, shall be made in the manner heretofore used and accustomed in such courts respectively, save and except that the jurors shall be returned from the body of the county . . . and shall be qualified according to the Act.

PRECEPT

Before the judges of assizes go to their circuit they issue their precept, signed and sealed, to the sheriff, to cause all persons bound to attend at the assize to appear before them on an appointed day, and requiring him to return a competent number of good and lawful men of the body of the county, qualified as jurors according to law.

The precept in relation to Assizes directs jurors to be summoned for the trial of all issues, whether civil or criminal, which may come on for trial at the Assizes.

The precept which the clerk of the peace has to send to the sheriff in respect of Quarter Sessions has to be signed by two justices of the peace and must be sent to him within a reasonable time before the opening of the session, 21 days being generally considered as reasonable for this purpose. The purport of the precept is similar to that issued for Assizes except that in the case of Quarter Sessions there is, of course, no question of jurors being summoned for the trial of civil cases. The summoning of jurors is the same whether it be for a general sessions of the peace or for adjourned Quarter Sessions.

The actual wording of the precept serves to remind one of the antiquity of Quarter Sessions and the following extracts illustrate this, the actual heading being:

> Of our Sovereign Lady the Queen, assigned to keep the Peace in the County aforesaid, and also to hear and determine divers Felonies, Trespasses, and other Misdemeanours in the said County committed TO THE SHERIFF OF THE SAME COUNTY GREETING ... [the date of the Sessions is then set out together with the place and time of hearing; then come the requirements] ... a competent Number of good and lawful men and women to try the issues ... to make known to all Justices, Coroners, Keepers of Gaols, Constables, Bailiffs, and other Officers, Keepers of the Peace ... that they be there ... [and finally a command that] the sheriff will proclaim throughout the county in proper places the aforesaid Session of the Peace to be holden at the time and place aforesaid and do yourself attend with your Bailiffs and other Officers to carry out your respective offices.

Since the Assize courts deal with more complicated cases than those that are dealt with by Sessions, it naturally follows that the length of time for which the services of jurors are required is much longer at those courts. It is not at all unusual for an assize case to last for several weeks — the outstanding example has, of course, been the recent train robbery trial at Aylesbury — with the consequent prolonged dislocation of the juror's ordinary routine. One important factor, however, may serve to mitigate the disturbance to their personal routine, and that is the fact that not infrequently judges of assizes exempt jurors who have been subjected to the ordeal of a prolonged trial from further jury service for life.

It is at once apparent that many of the duties which at one time, when transport and communications were somewhat slower than they are today, were imposed on the sheriff, are now undertaken by the clerk of assize or the clerk of the peace. The main duty which rests with the sheriff in connection with the precept is to make sure that Assizes or Quarter Sessions are supplied with an adequate panel of jurors.

JURY PANEL

It is actually the under-sheriff of a county who is responsible for seeing to the empanelling of jurors. The size of the panel depends on a variety of factors, the number of prisoners awaiting trial in any particular calendar at Assizes or Sessions, the number of courts which are available for trying the cases, and the likely duration of the assize or session. Allowance has always to be made for some wastage, and it may well prove necessary, in order to have an effective panel of 100 jurors, to summon nearly 150. Illness, holidays, genuine business excuses and various other reasons are usually responsible for reducing the panel even before the time arrives for another spate of excuses to be sorted out at the court. The usual practice nowadays is for the under-sheriff to consult the clerk of the court well in advance of the opening date of the assize or session and he will be given an idea whether more than the usual number of jurors will be required for the ensuing calendar.

JURY EXCUSES

The sheriff can himself excuse any person from attending at the assize or session, if he is satisfied that the excuse is a genuine one. In the old days the sheriff had to justify these excuses to the judge or court, but nowadays it is an accepted practice for the sheriff to deal with these advance excuses himself and his decisions are never challenged. He may, however, be obliged to strengthen his panel by issuing more summonses, should there be too many seeking to be excused; or he may tell the jurors that their excuses will be dealt with at the court; in that event it will be necessary for them to attend in accordance with their jury summons. There are, however, certain categories of persons such as barristers, doctors and police who are exempt from jury service. Reference has already been made to the fact that it is often possible nowadays to postpone the attendance of jurors until a later date in the session, in which event it is the duty of the clerk of the assize or the clerk of the peace to write and inform each individual juror on what date his or her attendance at the court will be required. Local requirements at any particular session will, of course, determine to what extent if at all, it is possible to dispense with jurors, even for one day.

It is also helpful, whenever this is at all possible, to divide the jury panel into two or three groups, so that some report on the second day of the session and the others on the third or a later day. The use of jurors at Assize courts is, of course, regulated by the fact that the greater jurisdiction of those courts results in their dealing with more complicated and lengthier cases, than those which are dealt with at Sessions. Though circumstances may not permit this, a consideration which has to be borne in mind is the accommodation factor. One of the results of the great increase in criminal work during recent years has been to strain to the utmost the accommodation that is available for the use of the courts. The empanelled jury in each court presents no difficulty. It has, however, to be visualized that all the juries in all the courts in any building may require to consider their verdicts at the same time, in which event a separate room has to be found for each of the retiring juries; and such rooms have to be reasonably sound-proof. In addition, spare juries have to be available to take their places in court, and, above all that, an adequate supply of spare jurors has to be available in case of any challenges to jurors. From the above it will be seen that it is far from an easy matter to prevent a certain amount of waiting about for those who are summoned for jury service.

EMPANELLING JURIES

When the day on which jurors are to attend the court has been determined, the first duty is to call over the jury panel. The calling of jurors generally takes place on the first day of the assize or session. This is done by an officer of the court. It is done for two reasons, first, to make sure that no jurors who have been summoned are absent, other than those whose attendance has been excused by the sheriff or the clerk of the court, and, secondly, to enable any juror who may desire to be excused to say so, and then these excuses will be dealt with at once. Jury service can be a very irksome burden and the golden rule for dealing with jury excuses is to be kind whenever possible. Medical certificates should, unless there are very exceptional circumstances, be taken as conclusive, and the utmost consideration should be given to the "one-man" shopkeeper or business man and to women jurors who have to look after small children. Any juror who intimates that he is hard of hearing is generally best kept off a jury panel, and night workers also should be released. It is not always possible to assist jurors as much as one would like to do for the simple reason that, as a class, they are reluctant to let the jury officer know the facts which would be almost certain, if known, to result in their immediate release. If a juror informs the court in advance that he has arranged his annual holiday during the period for which he is called to serve, he is often excused from attending that particular session and allowed to attend a later session instead.

During the course of some 20 years of dealing with jurors one is bound to come across some excuses which remain in one's memory. I remember one occasion when a woman juror asked to be released, and, when I asked her what her trouble was, she informed me that she had four young children at home with the measles. She was sent back to her family as speedily as possible, with the advice that the next time when her family got measles or any other illness, if she wrote to the sheriff, it would save her a journey to Sessions and the possible risk of spreading the complaint among the rest of the jurors. On another occasion, having dealt with all the excuses, I noticed a little man hesitate when about to follow the rest of the jurors to their room, so I asked him if he wanted to be excused. His reply somewhat astonished me, when he said almost in a whisper "I don't know whether I ought to serve, as I have only just come out". I replied, thinking that he meant that he had just come out of hospital, to the effect that I hoped he was better. "No", said he, "I mean I have just finished my sentence". Whereupon I thanked him for letting me know and he was duly released. One further possibility needs to be referred to, and that is, should a juror know a prisoner, or know of his record, even by heresay, the juror ought himself to take steps to be excused from taking part in the trial of that prisoner.

The excuses having all been dealt with, the jury cards are put in the ballot box and shuffled. Juries are then empanelled by drawing out the cards one by one until a complete jury is composed, and repeating the process until there is a jury for each court that is sitting, together with a spare jury also for each court. The remaining jurors who have not been drawn out of the ballot box will be kept as reserve jurors and as soon as it is possible to release them for the day they will be allowed to go. Since every person who stands trial at Quarter Sessions or Assizes has a statutory right to challenge up to seven jurors without stating any reason, courts have to retain a reserve of jurors until such time as there is no longer any possibility of a replacement being required on the day in question (see challenge to jurors, p. 50).

PENALTY FOR NON-APPEARANCE

Any juror who fails to attend after he has been duly summoned for jury service is liable to be fined. The sheriff must, however, serve the jury summons at least 6 days before the day on which the juror's presence is required at Assizes or Sessions.

The practice at Sessions is for the names of any absent jurors to be called and, if there is still no appearance, then a fine is imposed subject to the conditions that, if during the current Sessions the juror can show just cause why he should not be fined, then the fine may be remitted. It often happens in these cases that the juror has gone away, and in very few cases are the fines collected. It has not, however, been unknown for a juror to consider it worth his while to pay the fine and thus escape jury service.

No statutory limit is placed on the amount which a juror is liable to be fined (except in the case of a juror who does not answer to his call, or who wilfully withdraws himself from the court, in which case the minimum penalty is a fine of £10). Most Assize courts and quarter Sessions impose a fine of not less than £5.

No fine imposed on a juror for non-attendance may be enforced for 14 days. A duty is imposed on the officer of the court to inform the juror in writing, and an opportunity must be given to him of forwarding an affidavit of the cause of his non-attendance with a view to the fine being remitted (see section 12 of the Juries Act, 1862). A judge of assize or chairman of quarter sessions has complete discretion as to remission.

Before the jury is brought into court in order to try prisoners, there is one further step that has to be taken, and that is that the prisoner has to be arraigned. It is desirable that this should be done before the jury are in court. If the indictment concerns only one defendant who is charged on one count, and he pleads not guilty, no harm is done if the jury are present in court to hear him do so. Where there are more persons than one charged on the same indictment or several counts are included in the indictment, it is most desirable to have the jury out of court whilst the pleas are taken. It would not be right for a jury to know either that one or more of the prisoners had in fact pleaded guilty *in toto* or that one or more of them had pleaded to some of the counts in the indictment. They may learn this during the course of the trial, but it is not right for them to get the information in advance so to speak.

CHALLENGE TO JURORS

Thus when the jury are brought into court, they find that the dock is already occupied by the prisoner or prisoners whom they are to try. The first thing that the clerk of the court has to do then is to inform the prisoner of his right to challenge any juror. Section 35 of the Criminal Justice Act, 1948, gives any person who is arraigned on an indictment for any felony or misdemeanour the right to challenge not more than seven jurors without cause, and any juror or jurors for cause. This is done to give the defendant an opportunity of selecting those persons who are to try him so he may be sure of a fair trial. Thus it will be seen that if the trial of three prisoners who are joined on the same indictment is about to take place, there is always the possibility that each one of them will exercise his right to challenge seven jurors without cause. This is one of the reasons why so many waiting jurors are required. Any challenges for cause are tried by the judge or chairman. It is most important that each defendant is given the opportunity of challenging each individual juror, and this opportunity must be given before the oath is administered to the juror in question.

Any judge of assize or chairman of quarter sessions before whom a case is or may be heard may, in his discretion, on an application made by or on behalf of the prosecution or the accused, or at his own instance, make an order that the jury shall be composed of men only or of women only, as the case may require. Further a woman juror may herself apply to be exempted from service on a jury in respect of any case by reason of the unsavoury nature of the evidence to be given or of the issues to be tried (see section 1, Sex Disqualification (Removal) Act, 1919). In practice such applications are for all male juries.

To ensure that the prisoner or prisoners have this right of challenge, the procedure is as follows: the jury bailiff having placed the jurors in the jury box, the clerk of the court then addresses the prisoner or prisoners in these words: "Prisoner at the Bar the names I am about to call over are the names of the jurors who are to try you. If you wish to object to any of them, you should do so as they come to the book to be sworn, and before they are sworn, and you shall be heard." It is most important that each juror should be called by name to ensure that the defendant has a chance to challenge each of the empanelled twelve. In most cases in which prisoners are defended by counsel defending counsel usually informs the clerk of the court if he is proposing to challenge some juror and this enables the clerk to have spare jurors available without any waste of time. Challenge of jurors is not a prerogative of the defence; the prosecution also are entitled to do so, although this is not done nearly as frequently by the prosecution as it is by the defence, and when it is done, the challenge takes the form of counsel for the prosecution saying, "Stand by for the Crown". In a recent decision of the Court of Criminal Appeal it was held that after his undoubted right of peremptory challenges (see section 35 (1) of the Criminal Justice Act, 1948), a defendant had no legal right to "stand by" a juror. Whilst so deciding, however, the Court of Criminal Appeal certified that a point of law of general public importance was involved in their decision, namely whether there was a legal right today in an accused to follow what is the right of the Crown in standing jurors by and not challenging for cause until the panel is exhausted. The House of Lords have now refused leave to appeal, and the decision of the Court of Criminal Appeal therefore remains unchallenged. The prisoners having been addressed as stated above, the clerk then proceeds to call out the names of the jurors, one by one, and as his name is called the juror rises to his feet and (unless he is affirming) with the testament in his right hand and the jury oath card in his left hand proceeds to read out the oath, which runs as follows: "I swear by Almighty God (or I do solemnly, sincerely and truly declare and affirm) that I will faithfully try the several issues joined between our Sovereign Lady the Queen and the prisoner(s) at the Bar, and give a true verdict (or true verdicts) according to the evidence." In the event of a juror desiring to affirm the judge or chairman, as the case may be, has to give his consent.

PUTTING IN CHARGE

The jury are now ready to be put in charge of the prisoner whom they are to try. The next step, therefore, is for the clerk to address the jury in the following terms:

> Members of the jury, A.B. (or A.B. and C.D., etc.) stand(s) charged in this indictment in Count 1 that on the . . . day of . . . in the County of . . . he received a suitcase knowing it to be stolen. To this indictment he has pleaded not guilty and it is your charge to say, having heard the evidence, whether he be guilty or not guilty.

The jury are now in charge of the prisoner, and unless they are discharged from giving a verdict, as may happen on occasions for some technical reason, in which event the judge or chairman will discharge them from giving a verdict, the result of the trial rests upon their verdict of guilty or not guilty, as the case may be. Should the prisoner change his plea during the course of the trial and plead guilty, since he is in charge of the jury, the clerk will still have to take the verdict of the jury, and it is for them to return a verdict of guilty.

Similarly, if the prosecution decide to offer no evidence against a prisoner, the jury will be told by the judge or chairman that, as there has been no evidence offered by the prosecution, only one verdict is open to them, and they will duly find the prisoner not guilty. The reason for this formal procedure is that every defendant in such a case is entitled, if he insists, on being acquitted by a jury. Once this has taken place, he cannot be further charged with that particular offence. It sometimes happens when a prisoner pleads guilty to some of the counts on an indictment and not guilty to other counts, that the prosecution are willing to accept the plea as tendered; in which event it is the usual practice to apply for the counts to which he has pleaded not guilty to remain on the file and the indictment is then marked as regards those counts, "not to be proceeded with without leave of this court or of the Court of Criminal Appeal" — this procedure prevents the prosecution from reviving the counts left on the file, should the occasion require it, except with such leave.

CONSIDERING VERDICT

The trial then proceeds to the summing up by the judge or chairman, who will summarize the principal facts, explain the law in the charge in relation to those facts, remind the jury that they are the sole judges of matters of fact and that the burden of proving the guilt of the accused to their satisfaction rests fairly and squarely on the prosecution. He will then invite them to retire and consider their verdict or verdicts as the case may be. He will, probably, inform them of the desirability of electing one of their number as a foreman. Before the jury leave the court the jury bailiff, who nowadays is usually a police officer, is sworn on the following oath: "I swear by Almighty God that I will keep this jury in some quiet and convenient place. I will not suffer anyone to speak to them, neither will I speak to them myself, unless it be to ask them whether they are agreed on their verdict, without leave of the court."

Sometimes a jury retire to consider their verdict and after a long period of time there is still no sign of their being able to agree. It is a wise practice for the clerk to make a note of the exact time when a jury retire to consider their verdict. My own experience is that it is unwise to interfere with them in any way until they have been out of court for at least an hour. A jury having started their deliberations at say twenty minutes past twelve, when one o'clock is reached without word from them, it is pertinent to know whether the court should be adjourned forthwith, leaving the jury to give their verdict after the adjournment, or whether there is a chance that, if given a few minutes longer, they might come to a decision, in which case the adjournment would be postponed until the verdict is taken in order that the jury might be released.

Speaking generally, however, it is almost certain that, if the jury bailiff is asked to inquire of a jury before the hour is up, as to how much longer they are likely to be before arriving at their verdict, the answer will be that they do not know. If, however, the question is posed after they have been out for an hour at least, it is very probable that the reply will be forthcoming to the effect that they will need another 5 minutes. It is an axiom that, the longer a jury are in coming to their decision, the better are the prospects for an acquittal. I would add, however, that especially in motoring cases, there is also the likelihood of a failure to agree. It is the practice for a judge or chairman to ask a jury who have intimated that they are unable to agree on their verdict, whether they would like any further assistance; and also to point out to them the unfortunate consequences should they fail to agree. In such an event a fresh trial has to be ordered with all the expense involved both to the defendant and the prosecution. A judge or chairman's powers at this stage are extremely limited, and, if he exceeds them, the Court

COMMUNICATIONS TO JUDGE OR CHAIRMAN

When the summing up is completed, the jury bailiff takes the jury to their retiring room. On retiring, a jury are always entitled to take with them any of the exhibits which have been produced during the course of the hearing. Should the jury at any time after they have retired to consider their verdict desire to have further guidance from the judge or chairman, they should be brought back into court, the prisoner or prisoners brought back into the dock and counsel for both the prosecution and the defence should also be present in court. This is very important, as the prisoner is entitled to know about any communication which may be made by the jury to the judge or chairman. Should the request be merely formal, such as asking for a further exhibit in addition to those which they took out of court with them, there will be no need to bring the jury back into court. Similarly, if the matter which they desire to clear up is one that can be answered with a simple yes or no, this can be done by the jury writing the question down on paper and the judge or chairman doing the same with his answer. Even in these instances, however, the judge or chairman should read out the question and answer on his return to court, and before the jury give their verdict. The purport of the communication then finds its way on to the shorthand note of the court proceedings.

It sometimes happens that during an adjournment of a trial a juror is taken ill and cannot attend the adjourned hearing. Section 15 of the Criminal Justice Act, 1925, envisaged this situation and enacted the following provision:

> Subject to assent being given in writing by or on behalf of both the prosecution and the accused and so long as the number of its members is not reduced below ten,* the jury will be considered as remaining for all the purposes of the trial properly constituted, and the trial shall proceed and a verdict may be given accordingly.

*See, however, Criminal Justice Act, 1965 (see p. 136).

This procedure must, however, be strictly observed; should the prisoner object to the trial proceeding with less than 12 jurors, the judge or chairman will be left with no alternative but to discharge the remaining jurors from giving a verdict and the trial will have to be restarted before a new and full jury. It is also important that the consent be given in writing.*

Illness is not the only ground on which a trial can be allowed to proceed with less than 12 jurors. The section of the Act is phrased broadly and covers "any other reason", the whole object being to try to prevent the waste of time and public money which results from a trial having to be started all over again. Bad weather and transport difficulties have been held to be a sufficient ground for discharging a juror. The prisoner should be in court when the question of proceeding with less than 12 jurors is raised.

The court has the power to discharge a juror for misconduct. It is usual for a judge of assize or a chairman of quarter sessions to warn a new jury when they are trying their first case at the sessions, and the case has to be adjourned either for the luncheon interval, or until the next day, to be particularly careful not to talk to anyone connected with the case or to anyone outside their number about the case, since this would mean they would have to be discharged from giving a verdict and the trial would have to be started all over again.

Once a jury have retired from court to consider their verdict, they are "enclosed" in a convenient place appointed for that purpose, and once so enclosed they must not separate or leave the place appointed for their deliberation without the special permission of the court, which should only be given in case of evident necessity.

TAKING OF VERDICT

Be it short or be it long, the time comes for the jury to return to court and announce their verdict. It is of the utmost import-

*Since the 5th September 1965 this procedure has only applied in trials for murder or any capital charge (see Appendix I, p. 136).

ance to make absolutely certain that the 12 members who return to court are the same 12 who tried the case. Accordingly when they have returned to their seats in the jury box, the clerk of the court will then proceed to call on each individual juror to answer to his or her name, and not until he has satisfied himself that all is in order will he proceed to take the verdict.

He will then ask the jury whether they are all agreed on their verdict, and it is the practice for the foreman to answer on their behalf; having been assured on this point, the clerk will then ask them whether they find A.B. guilty or not guilty on count 1, and similarly on any other counts (other than alternative counts). Having dealt with the whole indictment in this way, and in the event of more than one prisoner being involved, with each of the prisoners separately, he will ask one final question to the effect "and that is the verdict of you all". The verdict of the jury has to be unanimous — one dissentient suffices to prevent agreement and result in the necessity for a retrial.

Further, the verdict of a jury must be clear and unambiguous. In the event of a verdict not being clear, it is the duty of a judge or chairman to take steps in order to clear up any ambiguity which may arise; and if necessary, he may give the jury a further direction in law. In order to obtain an unambiguous verdict, a judge or chairman is entitled to question a jury as to the meaning of their verdict. A jury are also allowed to add a rider to their verdict if they desire to do so — for instance, recommending the defendant to mercy — but this practice has of recent years tended to become less usual.

In all criminal cases a jury has a right to find a special verdict. Such verdict must, however, state positively the facts themselves. If consequent on an appeal to the Court of Criminal Appeal resulting from a special verdict by a jury at Assizes or Quarter Sessions, the Court of Criminal Appeal consider that a wrong conclusion has been arrived at by the convicting court, on the effect of the verdict, the Court of Criminal Appeal may, instead of allowing the appeal, order such conclusion to be recorded as appears to be in law required by the verdict, and pass such sentence in substitution for the sentence passed at the trial as may be warranted by law.

The Court of Criminal Appeal has laid down that special verdicts should be obtained only in the most exceptional cases. One such case which arises on occasion is, with regard to the question of insanity.

Prior to the 31st August 1964 when the Criminal Procedure (Insanity) Act, 1964, came into force, the question as to whether an accused person was fit to plead and stand his trial was an issue to be determined by a jury, and if the jury so held, the trial was not proceeded with, the accused person being detained in custody during Her Majesty's pleasure.

That Act laid down the procedure which now has to be followed, where any question as to the accused's insanity may be involved. The main difference being that this issue is no longer one to be determined as a preliminary matter, but may be raised, subject to certain conditions, during the course of the trial. Should the jury be satisfied that the accused is in fact insane the special verdict which they now have to return is "that the accused is not guilty by reason of insanity".

Should, however, a jury come to the conclusion that the accused is not insane, then it is necessary for a fresh jury to be empanelled in order to try the charge on which the accused has been committed for trial.

The criticism to which the old procedure was subject, namely that the guilt or innocence of an accused person who was found unfit to plead and stand his trial was never established, is therefore no longer valid.

The finding of the jury on this issue will be recorded by the clerk of the court on the indictment.

There is one other form of special verdict which is required of juries and this is in connection with indictments containing counts of larceny and receiving as alternative offences. Since a prisoner cannot, on the same facts, be found guilty on both counts in such an indictment, the Court of Criminal Appeal have directed that in such a case the verdict of the jury should be taken in the following manner "Do you find A.B. guilty either of stealing a bottle of whisky or of receiving the bottle of whisky knowing it to be stolen, or not guilty of either?" If the jury say not guilty, that is the end of the matter; should they say guilty, the clerk of the court will ask the further question "Guilty of which?" and the jury will say stealing or receiving, as the case may be.

The point of this is that on an appeal to the Court of Criminal Appeal that court can substitute a verdict on that count on which the jury have not given a verdict, whereas if the jury has found the defendant guilty on one count and not guilty on the other, the matter having been disposed of by the jury, the Court of Criminal Appeal cannot deal with the count on which the defendant has been found not guilty.

On the subject of jurors it is interesting to note that, with a view to economizing in manpower during the Second World War, the size of the juries at Quarter Sessions and Assizes was reduced to seven, except in murder trials. Whether it was a coincidence or not, the fact remains that, while the size of the jury remained at this figure, disagreements were practically unknown. The volume of work was, of course, very much less. However, as soon as the jury was restored to its pre-war figure of twelve, disagreements began to appear again. During these years the age for jury service was raised from 60 to 65, and many of those who are connected with Assizes and Quarter Sessions are of the opinion that this particular age group, i.e. 60 to 65, could still be of material assistance to the courts, had not the age limit been reduced after the war to the earlier one of 60.

PAYMENT OF JURORS

Up to the year 1949 jurors were entirely unpaid for their services. This did not help those responsible for dealing with the excuses which were put forward; indeed, on some occasions it seemed as if they all with one accord made excuse. Prisoners were entitled to be tried and so the necessity arose of sifting the chaff from the corn. It was not difficult to find out the pseudo-deaf juror, but other excuses had to be most carefully considered. The problem was sometimes solved by an offer of service at a later date.

However, in 1949 an Act was passed whereby jurors were enabled to claim for three things; first, their travelling expenses in coming to the court in order to perform their jury service; secondly, compensation for loss of earnings; and, thirdly, subsistence allowance to cover the cost of meals whilst performing these duties. Before 1949 I remember one occasion when a jury who had retired to consider their verdict asked if they could be supplied with tea and biscuits. A kindly chairman agreed at once without consulting the clerk. Some days later the question arose who was to pay for the teas which had been supplied to the jury! That could not happen now, as the jury would pay out of their subsistence allowance.

Actually it was section 1 of the Juries Act, 1949, which enacted that persons who serve as jurors shall be entitled to be paid in accordance with prescribed scales: (a) travelling and subsistence allowances, (b) compensation for loss of earnings (to include any additional expense to which they would not otherwise have been subject), provided that where the period of time over which earnings are lost is not more than 4 hours, the amount to be paid shall not exceed the sum of 10*s.* or where the period of time is more than 4 hours shall not exceed the sum of 20*s.* The amount due to a person serving as a juror has to be ascertained at Assizes by the clerk of assize, at the Central Criminal Court by the clerk of the court, and at Quarter Sessions by the clerk of the peace.

The prescribed scales mean "prescribed by Regulations made by the Secretary of State with the consent of the Treasury".

Section 2 enacted that the amount due to a person by way of payment in respect of jury service shall be ascertained, in the case of Quarter Sessions, by the clerk of the peace.

Section 3 lays down that the appropriate local treasurer shall pay the amount shown on an order duly made out by the clerk of the peace out of the appropriate local fund, and section 7 lays a duty upon the county treasurer to cause some person to attend sessions on his behalf for the purpose of paying any such orders.

The Juries Act, 1954, repealed the provisions of the proviso to subsection (1) of section 1 of the Juries Act, 1949, the repealed proviso being replaced by the Juror's Allowance Regulations, 1954 (1954, No. 1627), which laid down the travelling allowances to which a juror is entitled as follows: (1) third class fare if travelling by railway, (2) where no public transport is available, the amount actually paid for a hired vehicle or 1s. 6d. a mile, (3) travel by private conveyance, a rate not exceeding 6d. per mile.

The 1954 Regulations also increased the subsistance allowances from 3s. 6d. for not more than 4 hours to 5s., and for more than 4 hours from 7s. to 10s.,* whilst compensation for loss of earnings was also increased from 10s. and 20s. as originally laid down in the 1949 Act to 15s. and 30s. respectively.

Finally, the 1958 Jurors Allowances Regulations further increased the loss of earnings figure to 20s. and 40s. respectively, and the railway travel from third class fare to second class fare, and these figures were again increased by the 1962 Regulations to 25s. and 50s. respectively.

Jurors, when they have completed their duties, are usually thanked by the judge or chairman for their services and told that, if they go to the appropriate place, they will receive the allowances which are due to them. Each juror is then handed a form and given instructions how to fill it in. The form consists of two parts, Part 1, in which the juror fills in his name in block letters, then follows (a) loss of earnings or additional expense incurred in attending the court on the following dates. He then fills in on a separate line each date on which he has actually attended the

*See, however, Jurors' Allowances Regulations, 1966, which increased these allowances to 6s., 12s. 6d. and 15s. 6d., respectively as from 14th February 1966.

sessions, putting against each date the amount of his claim. He then goes to (*b*) travelling expenses — railway and/or bus fare from . . . to . . . and return, and fills this in in the same way as he has done (*a*), then comes (*c*) subsistence allowances, which he also fills in in the same way.

Each juror's attention is then drawn to the back of the form where there is a space for him to fill in the name and address of his employers together with their telephone number.

This completes Part 1 of the form. Part 2 is in the form of a certificate which runs as follows:

> I DECLARE that I have actually and necessarily:—
> (a) suffered loss of earnings which I should otherwise have made;
> (b) incurred additional expense; for the purpose of enabling me to perform jury service and that the amount of such loss or expense is not less than the sum I have claimed.
> I DECLARE THAT THE FOREGOING STATEMENT IS CORRECT.

The juror then signs the certificate. It is most important to make sure that this certificate is signed before the clerk of the court authorizes payment by the county treasurer. There is, generally speaking, no way in which a juror's claim can be checked. It does, however, happen on occasions that claims are made for loss of earnings and on the position being checked with the employers it turns out that the claim is not well founded.

CHAPTER 4

Trial by Jury — Quarter Sessions

Pleas of guilty — Pleas of not guilty — Adjournments — Witnesses — Exhibits — Judgment of the court — Bail estreats — Additional cases taken into consideration — Corrective training and preventive detention — Quarter Sessions: Size of bench, Rota of justices, Applications to court, Breaches of probation orders and conditional discharges, Commitals for sentence, Appeals from magistrates' courts, Licensing

HAVING dealt with the preliminary hearing before the magistrates and taken due note of the necessary duties that have to be performed by the clerk to the justices in order to commit an accused person to Assizes or Sessions with a view to his trial by jury, we will now proceed to examine the position when all is set for such a trial to be begun.

It is inevitable that some of the duties which fall on a clerk of the court whilst Assizes or Quarter Sessions are engaged in the hearing of cases in which the defendant has pleaded not guilty will have already been referred to in the previous chapter on jurors. Further, it will only be necessary to make passing references to the duties of jurors for the same reason.

It is proposed, therefore, to start this chapter by dealing with certain factors which are common to trial by jury, whether that trial takes place before a judge of assize or a chairman of quarter sessions. Then, in the later stages of this chapter, attention will be drawn to some of the functions of Quarter Sessions which affect those courts only.

PLEAS OF GUILTY

In general the procedure with regard to an accused person who pleads guilty is the same whether he does so at an Assize court or at Quarter Sessions. The prisoner is first arraigned, that is to say the indictment, or a précis of it, is read out to him by the clerk of the court, and at the end of each count he is asked whether he pleads guilty or not guilty to that count. In the event of a plea of guilty being entered to each count (other than alternative counts) no difficulty arises. It sometimes happens, however, that a prisoner pleads guilty to some of the counts in an indictment and not guilty to the remaining counts; in which event it will be a matter for the prosecution to determine whether the judge or chairman should be asked to agree to the pleas being accepted as tendered and to allow the remaining count or counts to remain on the file. When such approval is given, the indictment will be marked accordingly, and the subsequent procedure will be the same as in the case of a prisoner who has pleaded guilty to the whole indictment.

Prosecuting counsel will proceed to outline the facts of the case and to call the officer who is in charge of the case to give evidence as to the defendant's antecedents and inform the court of any previous convictions which may have been recorded against him. Since the 1st February 1964, however, on which date section 16 of the Children and Young Persons Act, 1963, came into operation, any offence of which a person of or over the age of 21 was found guilty while he was under the age of 14 shall be disregarded for the purposes of any evidence relating to his previous convictions; proof of service of notices as to previous convictions under section 23 of the Criminal Justice Act, 1948, to give the court power to pass a sentence of corrective training or preventive detention, or under the Commonwealth Immigrants Act, 1962, which is a necessary preliminary to a recommendation for deportation being made by the court, will also be given at this stage where relevant.

The defendant or his counsel will then cross-examine the officer regarding the evidence he has given; after which the probation officer will be called to give a social inquiry report. Usually such reports are available in all cases in which it is known for certain in advance that the defendant proposes to plead guilty. In the case of late committals, however, such reports are not always forthcoming and it may be necessary for the court to respite judgment to a day later in the session in order that such a report may be made available to the court.

Similarly, in the case of persons who have not yet attained the age of 21, reports as to their suitability for Borstal training or detention centre training are produced, if available. Here again, however, in the case of defendants who have been on bail or who were committed for trial shortly before the opening day of an assize or sessions, it may be found necessary for the court to adjourn its judgment until a day later in the session.

All the information which is available to the prosecution having been produced to the court, which in the case of young persons may well include school reports, detention centre and remand centre reports in addition to those already mentioned, it is then the turn of the defendant, or his counsel on his behalf, to call any witnesses whom he may desire to give evidence on his behalf. Such witnesses may, of course, be subjected to cross-examination by counsel for the prosecution. The defendant or his counsel will then proceed to make a speech in mitigation with a view to pointing out to the court any reasons which he may consider are likely to induce the court to deal more leniently with the defendant by way of sentence.

There may, of course, be a variety of reasons why a court may desire to postpone its judgment, some of these have already been indicated; another quite frequent reason is when it becomes apparent to the court that it is desirable to have a medical, mental or psychiatric report on the defendant. Sometimes this necessity arises from the grounds placed before the court in mitigation; on occasions it may turn out that there is no merit in the alleged ground for mitigation, but the court will have had the satisfaction of knowing that the allegation has been thoroughly investigated.

Before passing from pleas of guilty to deal with pleas of not guilty, it is necessary to mention at this point a factor which is common to all pleas; and that is that when the offence charged on the indictment is a felony, before the prisoner is sentenced by the judge or chairman, it is the duty of the clerk of the court to call on the prisoner in words to this effect: "A.B. have you anything to say why the sentence of the court should not be passed on you according to law."

The prisoner should then be asked by the judge or chairman (if he is not represented by counsel) whether he desires to call anybody to speak on his behalf. Since in the case of an unrepresented prisoner he is called on as soon as the prosecution have presented all the facts to the court, it is important that the clerk of the court and counsel for the prosecution should make certain that the opportunity of calling witnesses on his own behalf is given to the prisoner, and, if necessary, remind the judge or chairman before he delivers his judgment.

There is just one other point which might be mentioned at this stage, since it applies with equal force whether a prisoner has pleaded guilty or been found guilty by the verdict of a jury; and that is that a judge of assize or chairman of quarter sessions has the power to vary a sentence he has imposed at any time during the period of the particular assize or session in the course of which he has imposed the sentence in question, until the Assizes or Sessions are completed by the signing of the document which is delivered to the gaoler as recording the sentences of the court. Usually this power is used in order to reduce a sentence which, on reflection, appears to be excessive.

PLEAS OF NOT GUILTY

Before proceeding to deal with the trial of a prisoner who has pleaded not guilty, this is a suitable time to mention a point in relation to indictments, namely applications to amend the indictment as drawn. The amendment called for may be of a substantial nature — such as the quashing of a count — or more trivial, such as correcting the name of the alleged owner of the property. Either the prosecution or the defence can make such an application, and the proper time for it to be made is before the prisoner has been arraigned. There is, however, power for any such amendment to be made at any time during the course of the trial. It is unlikely, however, that a judge or chairman — within whose discretion it always is whether to allow an amendment to be made — will consent to such a course during the actual trial if it appears to him that the defence will be prejudiced by it.

The prisoner or prisoners, as the case may be, having pleaded not guilty, they will be allowed their chance to challenge any jurors.

Before dealing further with the course of a trial one must refer here to a difference in procedure which takes place at Assizes as opposed to Quarter Sessions. When a full jury have been sworn in cases of treason and felony, the crier (at the Assizes) makes proclamation in the following form:

> If any one can inform my lords the Queen's justices, or the Queen's Attorney-General, on this inquest to be taken between our sovereign lady the Queen and the prisoners at the bar, of any treasons, murder, felony, or misdemeanour, done or committed by the persons at the bar or any of them, let him come forth and he shall be heard; for the prisoners now stand at the bar upon their deliverance, and all persons who are bound by their recognizances to prosecute and give evidence against the prisoners at the bar, let them come forth and give evidence, or they shall forfeit their recognizances. God save the Queen.

It is now, therefore, time to review the procedure in a trial by jury; the opportunity to challenge any member of the empanelled jury having been given to the prisoner, he is then put in the charge of the jury. This is done by the clerk of the court reading out the précis of the indictment and charging the jury in the way already indicated in Chapter 3.

At this stage the scene is then set for the trial to commence, and counsel for the prosecution will make his opening speech to the jury in the course of which he will outline the case against the prisoner. He will point out to the jury the nature of the offence or offences with which the prisoner is charged in the various counts of the indictment. He will then call the several witnesses who have been bound over on behalf of the Crown to give their evidence on behalf of the prosecution in accordance with the depositions which, as we have seen, have been taken down at the magistrates' court. Since the important matter of witnesses will be dealt with in a later section of this chapter, there is no need to go into any further details concerning them at this point. It only needs to be added that each witness who is called on behalf of the prosecution will be liable to be cross-examined on behalf of the defence and, finally, should it be thought necessary, re-examined by counsel for the prosecution.

Having called all his witnesses, prosecuting counsel will then close the case for the prosecution, and it will then be the turn of the defence to call their evidence (if any) on behalf of the accused person.

It is at this stage of a trial, when a prisoner is conducting his own defence, that the judge or chairman should inform him of his right to give evidence on his own behalf or to make an unsworn statement and to call witnesses and to address the jury. This warning is necessary because although section 1 of the Criminal Evidence Act, 1898, enabled a prisoner to give evidence on oath on his own behalf, this section also further enacted that: "Nothing in this Act shall affect . . . any right of the person charged to make a statement without being sworn."

This right to make an unsworn statement is in fact quite often exercised by prisoners; and it is a not infrequent practice for counsel appearing on behalf of the defence, when an unsuccessful submission in law has been made during the course of the hearing, not to call his client to give evidence, but to rely on his address to the jury, and in the event of a conviction pursue the point of law by way of an appeal to the Court of Criminal Appeal.

In the event of a prisoner, however, desiring to give evidence on his own behalf, he will then proceed to do so, and will in due course be subjected to cross-examination by counsel for the prosecution. The defendant must, however, give evidence himself before he calls any witnesses on his own behalf, other than a purely formal witness. Where more accused persons than one are joined in an indictment it is the normal practice for them to give evidence in the order in which their names appear on the indictment. Each prisoner will give his own evidence and call any witnesses whom he may desire to call to give evidence on his own behalf, and will then close his case. The importance of this used to be that the order of the final speeches to the jury was affected by the fact whether a defendant gave evidence on his own behalf with or without the addition of other witnesses to support his case. Whereas a prisoner who himself only gave evidence preserved the right to have the last word with the jury, if he called witnesses (other than as to character), he lost this right and the prosecution were able, should they desire to do so, to make the final speech to the jury.

The order of speeches has, however, since the 10th July 1964, been affected by the provisions of the Criminal Procedure (Right of Reply) Act, 1964. That Act provided that upon the trial of any person on indictment (*a*) the prosecution shall not be entitled to the right of reply on the ground only that the Attorney-General or the Solicitor-General appears for the Crown at the trial, and (*b*) the time at which the prosecution is entitled to exercise their right to reply shall be after the close of the evidence for the defence and before the closing speech (if any) by or on behalf of the accused.

The effect of this statute was, therefore, to vary the procedure in a trial on indictment as previously laid down in section 2 of the Criminal Procedure Act, 1865, and section 3 of the Criminal Evidence Act, 1898.

The whole of the evidence having been completed — and it

should be pointed out that a judge or chairman has a right to allow other evidence to be called, or for a witness who has already given evidence to be recalled in order to clear up any matter that may have arisen since he gave his evidence — and the speeches completed, the judge or chairman will then proceed to sum up the case to the jury, and at the end of his summing up will ask them to consider their verdict. In some cases where the evidence is very clear, juries are able to agree on their verdict without having to retire from the court; the more usual practice, however, is for them to retire from the court and follow the procedure outlined in Chapter 3.

The final stage of a trial by jury, in the event of the defendant being found guilty, is the same as that in the case of a plea of guilty, save that prosecuting counsel does not in this instance, have to outline the facts.

ADJOURNMENTS

It frequently happens both at Assizes and at Quarter Sessions that a trial cannot be completed in one day. All such courts have the power to adjourn a part heard case from one day to another and in the event of a trial not being completed during the session in which it started, from that session to the next one. This arises quite often at the Central Criminal Court, but the work at Quarter Sessions is arranged so as to avoid this necessity arising, whilst a long case at Assizes other than the Central Criminal Court is dealt with at a special assize.

In the event of a trial being adjourned from one day to the next day, provided that the prisoner or prisoners were committed for trial on bail, either in their own recognizances or with a surety or sureties, and they are allowed bail for the adjournment on the same terms as before, no documents will be required to be signed. Should, however, the terms of the bail be varied, or a different person substituted as a surety, then the bail form will require to be endorsed anew. The bail form will have been received originally from the clerk to the committing justices if bail was granted on the committal; or from the governor of the prison to which the lower court committed the prisoner to await trial, if bail was granted after the conclusion of the proceedings before the magistrates, by the judge in chambers on a special application to him.

Applications are frequently made to a High Court judge to grant bail: but when it is known that an assize or sessions to which a prisoner has been committed for trial is due to start in a short time, or has actually started, the application is referred by the High Court to the trial court. In this event on receipt of the application form, the clerk of the court should either enter the case for early trial or, if that is not possible, he should notify the prosecuting solicitor in order that the officer in charge of the case may be present in court and deal with the matter of bail as an urgent priority; and if in the event the application is refused, it may be possible to get a comparatively early date fixed for the trial.

Although an official shorthand note is a statutory requirement with regard to the proceedings in court at both Assizes and Sessions, the official basis of the proceedings is, however, the indictment. It contains the charges against the accused, and, as set out in Chapter 2, it is signed by the clerk of assize, the clerk of the peace or the proper officer of the court. On arraignment the clerk of the court will have entered the plea, and on the commencement of the trial, the name of the judge or chairman, and in due course the date or dates on which the trial takes place. On the jury arriving at their verdict, he will record that verdict on the indictment, and, in the event of a conviction and the accused asking to have additional cases taken into consideration, this further fact will be duly recorded. The clerk of the court will attach to the indictment a copy of any such additional cases, so that the copy is available for the Court of Criminal Appeal.

The procedure regarding the proving of previous convictions, in order to qualify the accused person for corrective training or preventive detention, will be fully dealt with later on in the present chapter, and, if the indictment has charged a felony, the clerk of the court will duly call on the accused and ask whether he has anything to say before the sentence of the court is passed on him.

Earlier on reference was made to the proclamation at Assizes, and it is a suitable ending to this portion of the present chapter to set out the procedure on the rising of the court at Quarter Sessions. The usher pronounces the adjournment of the court by proclamation which runs as follows:

> All manner of persons who have anything further to do at the General Sessions of the Peace for the County of . . . , let them depart hence and give their attendance here on . . . the . . . day of . . . at . . . o'clock in the forenoon.
> God save the Queen and this honourable Bench.

The adjournment may be to the next day, from Friday to the following Monday, or to the next quarter or intermediate session, as the case may be, or it may even be generally without fixing any specific date.

WITNESSES

The witnesses who may be called on behalf of the prosecution can be divided into three categories. The first comprises those who are bound over by recognizance to appear at the trial and give evidence (see section 5 of the Magistrates' Courts Act, 1952, and rule 6 of the Magistrates' Courts Rules, 1952). The second comprises those witnesses who have been conditionally bound over. The witnesses who fall into this category are those whose attendance at the trial appears to the magistrates' court to be unnecessary by reason of anything contained in any statement of the accused, or of the accused having pleaded guilty to the charge, or of the evidence of the witness being merely of a formal nature.

It is laid down in section 13 of the Criminal Justice Act, 1925, that before any deposition of a conditionally bound witness may be read as evidence, it must be proved either by certificate or on oath that the deposition had been taken in the presence of the accused and that he had full opportunity of cross-examining the witness, and that the deposition must purport to be signed by the justice before whom it is purported to have been taken. These matters should be checked upon receipt of the documents from the clerk to the justices, and in order completely to satisfy the requirements of the statute, the clerk of the court when reading the depositions should make sure that the deposition has been signed by the justice and that the necessary certificate is attached thereto.

The third category of witness comprises those who are known as additional witnesses. These consist of witnesses who did not give evidence before the magistrates' court, but concerning whom notice has been served by the solicitor for the prosecution on the defence and the court. The notice will state that, in addition to the evidence given at the magistrates' court, further witnesses may be called to give evidence at the trial, and will set out the name or names of such witnesses and the substance and effect of such evidence.

The clerk to the committing justices will sign a form setting out the names, addresses and occupations of all witnesses whose attendance at the trial appears to the committing court to be unnecessary, and who have accordingly been bound over to attend the trial conditionally. The Court of Criminal Appeal has directed that this form should be attached to the depositions, even if it is a "nil" return, i.e. no witnesses having in fact been conditionally bound over to attend the trial.

When the prosecution desire to place the evidence of a witness who has been conditionally bound over before the jury, prosecuting counsel will ask the judge or chairman if the evidence of that witness can be read to the jury. If a new jury are trying the case, the judge or chairman will doubtless proceed to explain the procedure to them, and the clerk of the court will then read the deposition. In some magistrates' courts it is the practice to have the depositions taken down by typewriters and others continue to take them in longhand, in the latter case, the clerk of the court will read from a typed copy and he will hand the original to the judge or chairman so that he can check the reading.

It sometimes happens, however, either because a prisoner who was expected to plead guilty, in fact pleads not guilty, or because the prosecution or the defence request the presence in court of a witness who has been conditionally bound over, that some or all of these witnesses have to attend court and give their evidence on oath in the same way as those witnesses who have been bound over in the normal manner. The procedure for ensuring the attendance at Assizes or Quarter Sessions of a witness conditionally bound over is laid down in rule 7 of the Magistrates' Courts Rules, 1952, and is to this effect:

> if the prosecutor or the person committed for trial gives notice, at any time before the opening of the Assizes or Quarter Sessions at which that person is to be tried (to the clerk of the magistrates' court that committed him), or at any time thereafter to the Clerk of the Court, that he wishes the witness to attend at the trial, the clerk to whom the notice is given shall forthwith give notice in writing to the witness that he is required so to attend in pursuance of his recognizance.

Provision is also made for the clerk to notify the witness, in such manner as may be most expedient, thus covering the possibility of notice being received too late for the clerk of the court to notify the witness by letter at his last known address.

In a criminal trial the presiding judge has the right to call a witness not called by the prosecution or the defence and without the consent of either, if in his opinion this course is necessary in the interests of justice.

This may be done even after the close of the case for the prosecution; cross-examination of such a witness, whether by the prosecution or the defence, being only by leave of the judge. But in no case should a witness be called after the jury is enclosed.

Trial by Jury — Quarter Sessions

Similar considerations arise regarding the calling of a witness whose name is on the back of the indictment but who is not called by the prosecution.

EXHIBITS

In Chapter 2 reference has been made to the fact that clerks to justices have a duty to forward the originals of any statements or exhibits which have been put in evidence, either by the prosecution or the defence, during the course of the hearing before the magistrates. Rule 8 (c) of the Criminal Appeal Rules, 1908, laid down that a list of exhibits should be compiled on a set form, containing the following columns of information: column 1, No. of the exhibit; column 2, a short description of the exhibit; column 3, whether produced by the prosecution or the defence; and column 4 directions of the judge of court of trial with name and address of person retaining exhibit. This form has to be signed by the clerk to the committing justices. In general, only documents, such as written statements by the accused, letters, contracts and other similar exhibits, are retained by the clerk to the justices and forwarded on to Assizes or Sessions. Any other exhibits, such as bank-notes or bulky things such as cartons of goods, motor-cars, etc., are retained in the custody of the police who are responsible for producing them in court as and when required.

Exhibits are a most important feature of the duties of the clerk of the court during the hearing of a trial. The full definition of "exhibits" as laid down in the Criminal Appeal Rules, 1908, will be found in Chapter 5.* Exhibits are apt to be handed around from witness to judge or chairman, to counsel and the jury; and it behoves the clerk to keep a strict eye on them, since it is his responsibility to see that they are all available for the possible use of the Court of Criminal Appeal at the end of the trial. There is one further opportunity when exhibits may go astray, and that is when they are taken out to the jury's retiring

*See p. 129.

room. The safest course for the clerk to adopt is to ask the jury bailiff to hand in any exhibits that the jury took out of court with them on their return to court and before he actually takes the verdict of the jury. It has not been unknown for a juror to put an exhibit in his pocket, hoping to be able to keep it by way of a souvenir of his jury service.

Section 15 of the Criminal Appeal Act, 1907, enacts:

> Any documents, Exhibits, or other things connected with the proceedings on the trial of any person on indictment, who, if convicted, is entitled or may be authorized to appeal under this act, shall be kept in the custody of the court of trial in accordance with rules of court made for the purpose, for such time as may be provided by the rules, and subject to such power as may be given by the rules for the conditional release of any such documents etc.

Rule 8 empowers the judge of assize or chairman of quarter sessions to make any order he thinks fit for the custody, disposal or production of any exhibits in the case. This enables the judge or chairman to allow the return of vital documents, on an undertaking being given to produce them in the event of an appeal, before the statutory period of time in which an appeal can be entered has passed. It sometimes happens, too, that the defence desire to have access to some of the exhibits produced by the prosecution, either before or during the course of a hearing, in which event consent can be given only by an order made by the judge or chairman.

Apart from any direction given as just mentioned, the clerk of the court should not allow any exhibit to be taken out of the custody of the court until after the statutory period, which has been laid down as 10 days, has passed. This period of 10 days commences to run from the date of sentence or the verdict of the jury as the case may be.

Any additional exhibits which may be produced during the course of the trial, the clerk of the court should enter on the list which he has received from the clerk to the justices with the original depositions, and he (the clerk of the court) must also make sure that any new exhibits are duly marked.

Trial by Jury — Quarter Sessions

It may be found a helpful practice for the clerk of the court to check the exhibits attached to the original depositions whilst counsel for the prosecution is engaged in opening his case to the jury. He will then be prepared to hand out the exhibits as and when they are required by the various witnesses.

JUDGMENT OF THE COURT

The final stage of the trial has now been reached, and it only remains for the court to determine its judgment which is a matter entirely for the court; and the clerk, unless consulted by the judge or chairman, will take no part whatsoever. It sometimes happens, however, that a count or counts in an indictment carry considerably less punishment than the remaining counts (e.g. taking and driving away a motor-car without the consent of the owner, which carries a maximum penalty of 12 months' imprisonment), and in such cases, a timely reminder to the judge or chairman before sentence is pronounced may be helpful.

When the judgment of the court is pronounced, the clerk will record the sentence on the indictment and, if necessary, he will remind the judge or chairman to elucidate whether the sentences (in the event of conviction on more than one count in an indictment) are intended to run concurrently or consecutively. In a recent practice direction of the Court of Criminal Appeal the Lord Chief Justice stated:

> The attention of the court has been drawn to the fact that in many cases when the prisoner has been sentenced on more than one count, only one sentence, say three years imprisonment, is recorded on the indictment without indicating whether it is "concurrent on each count" or otherwise and, no doubt, this is because the Court has been concentrating on the total period of imprisonment appropriate, and has omitted specifically to say that it is intended to be concurrent on each count. While in the absence of any reference to a sentence being consecutive, it is no doubt intended to be concurrent, we think that this should, to avoid confusion, be expressly stated in the presence of the prisoner and entered on the indictment. The Clerk of the Court should therefore in such a case consult the Court before the prisoner leaves the dock, and ask the Court

to state expressly that the sentence is concurrent on all counts, or as the case may be and then make the appropriate entry on the indictment.

Convicted persons are sometimes already serving prison sentences before they are again convicted on fresh charges at Assizes or Quarter Sessions. In such cases the fresh sentence may be allowed to run concurrently with any unexpired portion of a sentence already in being, in which case the indictment will simply record "18 months' imprisonment" or whatever sentence is awarded by the court.

If, however, it is the desire of the court that any term of imprisonment then imposed is to run consecutively to an unexpired sentence, the clerk of the court will enter the record on the indictment as follows: "18 months' imprisonment to run consecutively to the total period of imprisonment to which he is already subject."

Section 17 of the Criminal Justice Administration Act, 1962, which came into force on the 18th July 1962, enacts that the length of any term of imprisonment, corrective training or preventive detention imposed by the sentence of any court shall be treated as reduced by any period during which the offender was in custody before the sentence by reason only of having been committed for trial, remanded after arraignment, or committed to Quarter Sessions by virtue of the provisions of sections 28 and 29 of the Magistrates' Courts Act, 1952.

The operation of the above section is automatic, and as a result, all accused persons, other than those who are already serving a sentence of imprisonment, will be allowed a calculated reduction from any sentence imposed by Assizes or Quarter Sessions. The clerk of the court does not have to calculate any reduction; that is a matter for the prison governor and — except in the case of the sentence being ordered to run consecutively to an unexpired sentence — the committal warrant signed by him will merely state the term of imprisonment.

BAIL ESTREATS

It sometimes happens that defendants who have been committed for trial to Assizes or Quarter Sessions and allowed bail, do not answer to their bail recognizances. The usual procedure in such a case at Quarter Sessions is for the chairman to issue a bench warrant for the arrest of the person in question and, in the event of a surety or sureties being involved, he or they will be warned that their respective recognizances are liable to be estreated. The bench warrant has to be signed by two justices of the peace, and once it has been issued the clerk of the peace will take no further steps in the case until he receives intimation from the police that the warrant has been executed. On receiving such intimation, he will take immediate steps to have the defendant brought before the court when, in the absence of a jury, the chairman will decide, having regard to any explanation the defendant may give, whether he should remain in custody awaiting his trial. If time permits, notice will be given also to the surety or sureties to attend. Should time be too short, such sureties will be given notice to attend on the date fixed for the trial. The usual practice with regard to the defendant's own recognizance is to await the verdict of the jury before dealing with the question of estreating. In the event of the defendant being convicted the chairman, should he decide to estreat the whole or part of the defendant's recognizance, may order any term of imprisonment which he orders in default of payment to run consecutively to any term or terms of imprisonment imposed on the count or counts in the indictment.

Although a bench warrant can be issued also by a judge at an Assize court, in which event he will sign the warrant himself, the alternative procedure of a certificate of indictment preferred and signed is the more normal process that is used at Assize courts. Section 12 of the Magistrates' Courts Act, 1952, enacts the required procedure as follows:

> If any person does not appear before a court of assize or quarter sessions to plead to an indictment against him before the end of the assize or

quarter sessions, as the case may be, at which the indictment is signed under Section two of the Administration of Justice (Miscellaneous Provisions) Act, 1933, the proper officer of the court may, on application being made to him by or on behalf of the prosecutor, grant to the prosecutor a certificate of the signing of the indictment.

On production of the certificate a justice of the peace for any county or borough in which any offence is charged in the indictment shall issue a warrant to arrest the accused and bring him before a magistrates' court for that county or borough.

It should be noted that whereas the certificate of indictment has a wider application, it can only be applied for on the last day of the assize or sessions to which the defendant has been committed; whilst a bench warrant, on the other hand, may be issued forthwith on any day during the course of the assize or sessions, but the authority of a bench warrant does not run outside the area of the county in which it is issued.

ADDITIONAL CASES TAKEN INTO CONSIDERATION

There is one further factor which may arise with regard to any accused person who either pleads guilty or is found guilty by a jury at Assizes or Sessions, and that is, that he may ask to have additional cases taken into consideration. In such instances the practice is for the officer in charge of a case to serve notice on the prisoner of a list of the further offences which he has intimated that he desires to have taken into consideration. These further offences are set out on a form giving the date, nature and place of each such offence and whether a warrant has been issued in respect of it. The prisoner will then endorse his desire to admit these cases by signing the form. The matter is brought to the notice of the court by prosecuting counsel asking the officer in charge of the case, while he is in the witness box giving his evidence, whether he knows that the prisoner wishes to have additional cases taken into consideration. The clerk of the court or judge has then to ask the prisoner if that is so, and it is his duty to put the matter to him in the following way: "A.B.

Trial by Jury — Quarter Sessions

do you desire to have . . . additional cases taken into consideration, as set out in the form supplied to you [should the prisoner not admit certain of the cases on the list, he will add with the exception of Nos. . . .]". He will then give an analysis of the list in some such words as "consisting of . . . cases of housebreaking . . . cases of shopbreaking etc." He will then ask the prisoner if he pleads guilty to those cases and desires to have them taken into consideration. It is no longer necessary for the cases to be put separately unless the prisoner desires further elucidation. As on some occasions a large number of such cases are in fact taken into consideration, the procedure has been materially shortened by the analysis method. The prisoner must, however, himself consent to such additional cases being taken into consideration, and cannot do so through the medium of his counsel.

On the prisoner having indicated his consent, the clerk of the court will then make the appropriate entry on the record or indictment as the case may be. The entry will be to the effect ". . . additional cases taken into consideration". He will also see that a copy of the list is attached to the indictment or record, so that it is available in the event of an appeal to the Court of Criminal Appeal.

The effect of this procedure, as far as the prisoner is concerned, is to ensure that no further action will be taken regarding the charges so taken into account. The court cannot, however, sentence the prisoner beyond the maximum sentence which is applicable to the offence on which he is charged on the indictment. The Court of Criminal Appeal has further laid down that only charges of a similar nature to those included in the indictment should be taken into consideration. The clerk of the court has also to make sure that no charges which are either triable summarily only, or in the case of Quarter Sessions are triable only at Assizes or charges relating to offences outside the United Kingdom, are allowed to be taken into consideration by the court. Usually copies of such offences are supplied to the court well in advance of the case coming on for trial. It does, however, occasionally happen that a long list is produced at the last minute, in which case there is no time for the clerk to make his analysis, and it may even be necessary, unless they happen to be all cases of a similar type, to go through them in more detail than would otherwise be the case. It has to be noted, however, that cases taken into consideration do not amount to convictions, so that if the main conviction is quashed, it is possible in law to prefer further charges in respect of the cases taken into consideration.

CORRECTIVE TRAINING AND PREVENTIVE DETENTION

Although it may well be that during the course of the next few years these particular forms of punishment, which came into being as a result of the Criminal Justice Act, 1948, may almost cease to exist for all practical purposes, they are still punishments that are open to Assize and Sessions courts, and this is the appropriate place to refer to them; further slight reference will be made when we come to deal with committals for sentence, but that is a matter which affects Quarter Sessions only.

The Criminal Justice Act, 1948, gave new powers of sentencing to courts of Assizes and Quarter Sessions in relation to the more hardened criminals who appear before them. This Act, whilst it abolished penal servitude, hard labour and prison divisions, enacted in section 21 two new powers of dealing with persistent offenders, namely corrective training and preventive detention, the latter replacing the old habitual criminal procedure. Section 22, which rendered discharged prisoners liable to notify their addresses to an approved society, was repealed by the Criminal Justice Act, 1961, as from the 2nd October 1961; thus this particular form of restriction was shortlived in its practical application.

If the prosecution desire to render a person liable to a sentence of corrective training or preventive detention, it is a prerequisite that notice must be served on the defendant and on the proper officer of the court, and the notice must be served at least 3 days before the trial. The Court of Criminal Appeal have held that "3 days" means three clear days. The clerk of the court has, therefore, to be alert, if notices are served within this period from the opening day of an Assizes or Sessions, to make sure that no such case is listed for hearing until the three clear days have elapsed. If this is not done, the notices will be ineffective and the court will not be able to deal with the prisoner under the provisions of section 21 (1) or 21 (2) of the 1948 Act. The defect in the time factor cannot be put right by adjourning sentence in order that notices can be served, since once the prisoner has been arraigned or brought before the court under the section, this appearance counts as the date of trial.

In the event of the court being supplied with a report from the Prison Department of the Home Office concerning the desirability or suitability of a sentence of corrective training or preventive detention being imposed on any prisoner, the clerk of the court should make sure that a copy is given either to the prisoner or, if he is represented by counsel, to his counsel. The Court of Criminal Appeal have directed that this fact should be recorded on the shorthand note of the proceedings. This became necessary because sometimes prisoners alleged, when appealing to the Court of Criminal Appeal against their sentences, that they had not in fact been given a copy of these reports.

With regard to medical reports, it is always a matter for the discretion of the judge or chairman whether these should be handed to a prisoner when he is unrepresented. It is, however, important that the clerk of the court should obtain the judge's or chairman's direction on this point. Reports handed into the court by probation officers, on the other hand, should always be handed to a prisoner or his counsel, as he is entitled to know their contents, and also, if he so desires, to cross-examine the probation officer on the contents of the report.

To revert to the position when notices have in fact been served, the officer in charge of the case will proceed to prove the service, and the clerk of the court will then read out the previous convictions as set out in the notices and ask the prisoner if he admits them. In the event of all or any of these convictions not being admitted, a jury will be sworn to determine the issue regarding such previous convictions. It is safe to say that although this procedure has been in operation since the coming into force of the 1948 Act, very few occasions have occurred when it has been necessary to have the fact of a previous conviction established by the verdict of a jury.

It should, however, be pointed out that this procedure does not apply to a person committed for sentence under the provisions of section 29 of the Magistrates' Courts Act, 1952, as in that event section 29 (5) of the Criminal Justice Act, 1948, enacts that this point is determined by the court and not by the verdict of a jury.

Having dealt with trials by jury in general, and covered the position at both Assizes and Quarter Sessions, it is proposed now to pass to certain features which are peculiar to Quarter Sessions as such.

QUARTER SESSIONS

Size of bench

Every Quarter Sessions has to sit at least four times a year, the four Quarter Sessions dates being known as County Days. Any sessions that are held between these four main dates are known as Intermediate Sessions.

I have already referred to the proclamations at Assizes and on the adjournment of the court at Quarter Sessions, and this is an appropriate place to set out the opening proclamation at sessions. On the entry of the chairman and lay justices into court, the usher calls out the Opening Proclamation as follows: "All manner of persons who have anything to do at the General

Quarter Sessions of the Peace for the County of . . . draw near and give your attendance. God save the Queen." This opening proclamation is repeated on each day of the sessions.

Up to a few years ago there was no limitation on the number of justices who could sit on the bench at any time at Quarter Sessions. This had two great disadvantages, first, that on the opening day of a Sessions the bench tended to become overcrowded, at least during the morning sitting; secondly, that after the first flush of enthusiasm had worn off, the attendance of lay justices was apt to become very thin. This was particularly the case as the calendars began to increase in size, and the number of days on which the attendance of lay justices was required began to expand from a matter of a few days to that of weeks. It was found that, whilst certain volunteers could be relied on, the number of these old regulars was strictly limited; thus it became more and more a case of driving the willing horse.

However, in 1950 rules were made limiting the size of the bench. These rules were made by virtue of the Justices of the Peace Act, 1949, section 13, and are called Justices of the Peace (Size and Chairmanship of Bench) Rules, 1950. The effect of these rules was to limit the maximum number of justices who could sit on the bench at Quarter Sessions to deal with a case, to nine (including the chairman). The legal quorum for the bench remained at two (London Sessions, by a special Act of Parliament, were able to sit without a lay justice) up to the 1st April 1965. The old County of London Sessions on that date became known as Inner London Sessions by virtue of the provisions of the Administration of Justice Act, 1964. Schedule 1 of that Act, however, gives power to the Lord Chancellor to enable a court of Quarter Sessions within the Greater London Area on application being made to him to allow a legally qualified chairman to sit on his own without a lay justice.

Rota of justices

The rules referred to in the last paragraph also laid down that within 6 months of their coming into force (the 1st January 1951) each court of Quarter Sessions should prepare and submit to the Lord Chancellor a scheme designed to secure that there shall be enough justices (not exceeding the maximum of nine) sitting to deal with cases brought before the court.

To cite an example in Middlesex, the rota which has been approved by the Lord Chancellor is worked on the basis of the Clerk of the peace allocating certain dates in each week of any Sessions to the various petty sessional divisions who in turn send a list of the names of the justices from their respective divisions together with the dates on which they will be able to attend Quarter Sessions. This arrangement is intended to result in an attendance at Sessions on each day of two justices for each court that is sitting. Even this arrangement was found liable to cause difficulties when cases that took more than one or two days to try fell to be heard, the lay justices being for the most part busy persons, and in addition having to attend their own petty sessional court by rota when called on. In fact, it was not unknown for a part-heard case to have to be restarted because the lay justice or justices who were present on the first or second day of the hearing were unable to attend on the further adjourned hearing. It was in order to prevent this that section 4 (5) of the Criminal Justice Act, 1962, became law, and it is now permissible for a chairman or deputy chairman of quarter sessions to sit alone in order to complete a trial under such circumstances as are enumerated above. This power, however, is strictly limited to an emergency. When it is known in advance that a particular case is likely to take some considerable time, every endeavour is made to find justices who are most likely to be available for the whole of the trial.

With a view to ensuring that newly appointed justices are made familiar with the duties of their office, the Lord Chancellor laid a duty on all magistrates' courts committees to prepare training schemes for the instruction of newly appointed justices. These schemes have in fact been in operation for several years. It has recently been announced that compulsory training is to be introduced for new magistrates.* While they are taking the course, they will not be able to adjudicate without special permission, and those who fail to complete the training within a specified period will have to resign.

The Lord Chancellor is also appointing a National Advisory Council to advise him on the instruction of magistrates and on how to improve present schemes. To this end a training officer has been appointed as a full-time member of the Lord Chancellor's staff.

This move follows an earlier one by the Lord Chief Justice of holding conferences with justices of the peace with a view to obtaining some uniformity of penalties as imposed by magistrates' courts without, of course, taking away the discretion to deal with each individual case on its merits.

Applications to court

At the commencement of the paragraph headed "Pleas of not guilty" reference was made to applications to amend the indictment as drawn. I now propose to make more specific reference to this point. The provisions of section 5 of the Indictments Act, 1915, are as follows:

> Where before trial or at any stage of a trial, it appears to the court that the indictment is defective, the court shall make such order for the amendment of the indictment as the court thinks necessary to meet the circumstances of the case, unless having regard to the merits of the case, the required amendments cannot be made without injustice, and may make such order as to the payment of any costs incurred owing to the necessity for amendment as the court thinks fit.

The above-mentioned section applies, of course, equally to both Assizes and Quarter Sessions. Once an amendment has been allowed, the clerk of the court should amend the indictment accordingly, and the judge or chairman will then initial the amendment.

*This now applies to all justices who are appointed on or after the 1st January 1966.

It follows, of course, that all such applications should be made in the absence of the jury. There is also the possibility, in cases where two or more prisoners are joined in the same indictment, that defending counsel will desire to make an application to the court to have separate trials. It is perfectly correct for the indictment to be drawn up with the prisoners joined, since it is always possible for counts or prisoners to be separated so as to result in separate trials, whilst it is impossible for persons who are indicted separately to be tried together. "Separately indicted, separately tried" is an unbreakable rule. The question whether a separate trial should be allowed is entirely one for the discretion of the judge or chairman, and here again the dominant factor which will govern his decision will be whether he is of opinion that the defence will be prejudiced if the application for separate trials is refused.

A repercussion of the large number of cases that involve offences in connection with motor-cars that are now dealt with by Quarter Sessions has led to a not unnatural spate of applications by persons who have been disqualified from holding or obtaining a driving licence with a view to persuading the court to remove the disqualification. There are really two different types of offenders who are concerned here; first, motorists who have been convicted as a result of charges resulting from their driving of motor-cars, and secondly those persons who have committed crimes such as shopbreaking and in the course of carrying out their crime have also made use of a motor vehicle which does not belong to them in order to assist them in the project. Before such an application is brought before the court, it is necessary to make sure that the applicant is entitled to make the application. The operative sections which apply are section 106 of the Road Traffic Act, 1960, and section 6 of the Road Traffic Act, 1962. The latter section enacts that a person who has been disqualified from holding a driving licence on or after the 29th May 1963 for a period of 2 years or less cannot make an application to the court to have his licence restored, or before one-half of the period of disqualification if it is less than 10 years or more than 4 years, and 5 years in any other case. As time goes on, therefore, this will result in fewer of these applications being made. Such as there are will relate to the longer periods of disqualification.

Provided that the necessary notice has been given and the minimum time has expired, the application is in order, and it usually happens that several of them are dealt with on the opening day of a session. It should be added that if a person who has been disqualified gives due notice that he intends to apply to the court to have his licence restored and fails to implement the application, the court cannot award costs against him since, until he puts in an appearance, there is no effective application before the court. The Court of Criminal Appeal has drawn attention to the desirability of applicants for restoration of licences giving evidence on oath.

Breaches of probation orders and conditional discharges

It is seldom that a session passes without the court having to deal with some breaches either of probation orders or orders of conditional discharge. With regard to the latter the period of conditional discharge is usually for the maximum of 12 months, whilst the period of probation orders varies between one and three years, the longer period being the more usual. It has to be borne in mind that Assize Courts and Quarter Sessions have no power to sentence a person for a breach of a requirement in a probation order, conditional discharge or bind over, as the case may be. The only power of sentencing for a breach of a probation order is that contained in section 8 of the Criminal Justice Act, 1948, which enables magistrates' courts to impose a fine not exceeding £10 for minor infringements. Assizes and Quarter Sessions when dealing with breaches of requirement are in fact sentencing the offender for the original offence in respect of which he was originally placed on probation or conditionally discharged. Since all probation orders are subject to regular review, it is always possible for Quarter Sessions or any court that places a person on probation to rescind an order before the expiry of the original period for which it was imposed, should circumstances justify such a course. Quarter Sessions, however, have no power to vary their own order, and should they desire to do so, the only way in which it can be done is by cancelling the old order and imposing a fresh probation order which will include the variation that the court desires to impose.

In each case the clerk of the peace will have sent notices to the offender in person if on bail, or to the governor of the remand home or prison to which he has been committed whilst awaiting his appearance at Quarter Sessions. Notices will also have been sent to any surety or sureties who may have entered into recognizances on behalf of the offender when he was originally put on probation.

It has been the practice of recent years, acting on a direction of the Court of Criminal Appeal, for the court to identify the offender and to ascertain whether he admits the original conviction and order and the subsequent breach. This is done in order to save the attendance at Sessions of a number of police officers.

Should a defendant not admit any of the above facts, it will be necessary for the case to be adjourned in order that the witness may be brought to court. Provided, however, that the defendant admits the above facts as put to him, then the officer in charge of the case will be called and will proceed to give the antecedents of the defendant. The probation officer will then submit his report to the court and the defendant will be enabled to ask him any questions that he may desire. It is not, however, every breach that consists in the commission of another offence; some consist in the probationer failing to carry out the specific requirements of the order. In this event the clerk of the peace will have to put to the probationer the exact term or terms of the order which the committing court have certified as having been broken by him.

It is not unknown that when a probation order is drawing near to the end of its period and the probationer commits a breach for which he is committed to Sessions, that by the time when he appears in court the probation order will have run its course. This, however, will not, apart from its mitigating effect, save the probationer from being liable to be sentenced, since it is the date of the actual breach which is the effective one to be considered. Provided that that date is within the period of the probation order, the breach can be effectively proved. It has to be borne in mind that the offender is not being sentenced for the breach but for the original offence in respect of which he was put on probation. There is power for magistrates' courts to deal with these breaches by way of a small fine; but this process relates only to minor infringements of the conditions of the probation order.

Committals for sentence

The Criminal Justice Act, 1948, together with the Magistrates' Courts Act, 1952, laid down a procedure by which persons who had been convicted before a magistrates' court and whom that court considered ought to be dealt with more severely than their own restricted powers of punishment allowed, should be committed in custody to Quarter Sessions for that court to determine the sentence. As we will see later, it is always open to such a convicted person to appeal to Quarter Sessions against his conviction at the lower court before he can be sentenced. The operative sections are sections 28 and 29 of the Magistrates' Courts Act, 1952, and sections 20 and 29 of the Criminal Justice Act, 1948. As these sections refer to two different categories of offenders, it is proposed to take one example of each. It has, however, to be remembered throughout that there are many Acts of Parliament whose provisions have to be borne in mind when a court of Quarter Sessions is dealing with such cases.

The tendency of Parliament during the past few decades has

been to restrict the powers of courts to imprison young offenders. Section 17 of the Criminal Justice Act, 1948, enacted that "a court of Quarter Sessions shall not impose imprisonment on a person under 15 years of age". This section also imposed a further curb by enacting that "no court shall impose imprisonment on a person under 21 years of age unless the court is of the opinion that no other method of dealing with him is appropriate", and further provided that "Where a court of Quarter Sessions imposes imprisonment on any such person, the court shall state the reason for its opinion that no other method of dealing with him is appropriate".

Section 2 (2) of the Criminal Justice Act, 1961, which came into force on the 1st August 1963, has further restricted the powers of Quarter Sessions to impose a term of imprisonment on young persons by substituting "seventeen years" for "fifteen years" as laid down in the earlier statute.

Sections 1–7 of the Criminal Justice Act, 1961, all of which came into force on the 1st August 1963, also have considerable bearing on the powers of Quarter Sessions, in sentencing persons under 21 years of age, the main feature, in addition to the one just mentioned, being the reduction of the qualifying age for Borstal training from 16 to 15. It also introduced two categories of imprisonment for those aged over 17 and under 21, i.e. either a maximum of 6 months or a minimum of 3 years, according to the fulfilment of certain qualifications as set out in section 3.

A sentence of 18 months' imprisonment can also be imposed in the event of certain conditions having been fulfilled, where there has been a previous sentence of not less than 6 months' imprisonment or the accused has served a sentence of Borstal training.

Section 18 of the Criminal Justice Act, 1948, first gave power to courts of Quarter Sessions to impose a sentence of detention in a detention centre once that court had been notified by the Secretary of State that accommodation was available. The

1961 Act has extended the powers of these courts to increase the maximum period of such detention from 6 months, as laid down in the Act of 1948, to 9 months in certain circumstances.

Having given a brief summary of some of the points which have to be borne in mind by a court of Quarter Sessions, I will now deal with the case of a person who has been committed to Sessions for sentence under the provisions of section 28 of the Magistrates' Courts Act, 1952. This procedure applies, if certain conditions are fulfilled, to a person who on the day of his conviction is not less than 15 but under 21 years old, the committal in this instance being with a view to Quarter Sessions considering a sentence of Borstal training as being appropriate. Such committals, however, are not necessarily confined to section 28; they can also take place by virtue of the provisions of section 29, provided that the offender is not less than 17 years of age.

Apart from those persons just referred to above, all persons who are not less than 17 years old can be committed in custody to Quarter Sessions for sentence under the provisions of section 29.

If the committal be by virtue of section 29 of the Magistrates' Courts Act, 1952, Quarter Sessions has the power to sentence the person so committed as if he had just been convicted on indictment. In the event of a committal by virtue of section 28 of the Magistrates' Courts Act, 1952, however, Quarter Sessions are not bound to order Borstal training, but can, if they like, deal with a person so committed in any way in which the magistrates could have dealt with him; and in that event the person so dealt with will not have a right of appeal unless he has been sentenced to Borstal training.

Having touched on the rather specialized committal under the provisions of section 29, which in effect enlarges the powers of punishment which are available to Quarter Sessions in the case of a person who is under the age of 21, I will now refer shortly to committals under this section in relation to persons who are 21 or older.

The effect of a person being thus committed to Quarter Sessions for sentence is that that court may deal with him as if he had just been found guilty by the verdict of a jury. This, of course, has the effect of rendering him liable to a much longer term of imprisonment or other punishment than would have been the case had he been dealt with at the magistrates' court. In this connection also notices may be served, where appropriate, to render such a person liable to be sentenced to a term of corrective training or of preventive detention or to be recommended for deportation. Since, however, this question has already been dealt with under the paragraph dealing with those punishments, there is no need to refer further to it at this stage.

Quarter Sessions are not bound, just because a person is committed to them under this section, to impose a heavier penalty than could have been inflicted by the magistrates; they may deal with such a person in any way that is within their powers, and as we will see later, the sentence finally imposed by Quarter Sessions will have a bearing on the defendant's right of appeal.

When a person is committed for sentence, no indictment has to be drawn up, but for administrative purposes (and the exact method may well differ in different courts) a record is kept which contains the charge or charges on which the prisoner has been committed; and on this record the clerk of the peace will duly enter the date of the hearing, the name of the presiding chairman and, in due course, the judgment of the court. The record will also include the fact, if it be so, that the prisoner asked to have further offences taken into consideration.

When a person who has been committed for sentence is called on, the clerk of the peace will ask him if he admits the facts of the conviction or convictions at the magistrates' court, together with the fact that on such and such a date he was committed to sessions for sentence. The date of conviction and the date of committal are quite frequently different, especially in section 28 committals where the magistrates often remand cases in order that further inquiries may be made. Provided that the prisoner admits the above facts, counsel for the prosecution will then proceed to open the facts to the court, and call the officer in charge of the case, who will give the antecedent history of the prisoner, and, if necessary, deal with the service of notices. Otherwise the procedure is the same as that already dealt with under the paragraph headed "Pleas of guilty". Should a report as to suitability for Borstal training be available to the court, a copy must be handed to the prisoner or his counsel.

Appeals from magistrates' courts

Having dealt with the trial procedure at Quarter Sessions, I now propose to deal with the working of Quarter Sessions with regard to the hearing of appeals from magistrates' courts.

Prior to the coming into force of section 4 (6) of the Criminal Justice Administration Act, 1962, on the 30th April 1962, appeals to Quarter Sessions were heard by a committee who were appointed annually by Quarter Sessions on nominations from the various petty sessional divisions of the county. Appeals could, therefore, only be heard by a bench composed of those persons who had been appointed as members of the Appeal Committee. Further, section 3 of the Summary Jurisdiction (Appeals) Act, 1933, laid down a minimum quorum of three or a maximum of twelve justices for hearing appeals at Quarter Sessions. This section has now been repealed, and as a result of this repeal a chairman of quarter sessions no longer has a casting vote when hearing appeals from magistrates' courts.

Section 4 (6) of the 1962 Act enacted that "any functions exercisable before the commencement of this Act [30.4.62] by an Appeal Committee appointed under section 7 of the Summary Jurisdiction (Appeals) Act, 1933, shall after the commencement of this Act be exercisable by the court by which the Committee was appointed". Provision is also made in subsection (7) for arrangements to be made to secure, as far as practicable, that when Quarter Sessions are dealing with a case on appeal from a juvenile court, not less than half the justices sitting are justices qualified to sit as members of a juvenile court, and of the justices sitting and so qualified, one is a man and one is a woman.

The Magistrates' Courts Act, 1952, section 83, which amended the Summary Jurisdiction (Appeals) Act, 1933, which itself had amended the Summary Jurisdiction Act, 1879, gives a general right of appeal to Quarter Sessions to a person if he pleaded guilty, against his sentence, or if he did not plead guilty, against the conviction or sentence, sentence being defined in section 83 (3) to include

> any order made on conviction by a magistrates' court, not being (a) a probation order or an order for conditional discharge; (b) an order for payment of costs; (c) an order under section 2 of the Protection of Animals Act, 1911; (d) an order made in pursuance of any enactment under which the court has no discretion as to the making of the order or its terms.

A prerequisite of an appeal is that the appellant shall, within 14 days after the day on which the decision was given, give notice of appeal to the clerk of the magistrates' court and to the other party. In the event of the appellant being in custody, the magistrates' court are empowered to release him on bail provided that he enters into satisfactory recognizances with or without a surety or sureties (section 89).

This power applies also in the case of an accused person who has been committed to Quarter Sessions for sentence under sections 28 and 29 of the Magistrates' Courts Act, 1952, in the event of such a person giving notice of appeal against his conviction.

Quarter Sessions may by their order confirm, reverse or vary the decision of the court of summary jurisdiction, or they may remit the matter with their opinion thereon to the court of summary jurisdiction or may make such other order in the matter as they think just. The powers of Quarter Sessions in this respect are, however, limited to the powers which the court of summary jurisdiction might have exercised. Quarter Sessions have, however, on dismissing an appeal against conviction, no power to commit to themselves for sentence under section 29 of the Magistrates' Courts Act, 1952. Quarter Sessions may also make such order as to costs to be paid by either party as they think just.

Section 2 of the Summary Jurisdiction (Appeals) Act, 1933, makes provision for a person who has been convicted of an offence by a magistrates' court and who desires to appeal to Quarter Sessions, to apply to the court at which he has been convicted for free legal aid.

If the magistrates' court are satisfied that the means of the applicant are insufficient to enable him to obtain legal aid and that it is desirable in the interests of justice that he should have free legal aid, the court may grant him an appeal aid certificate.

Should the court of summary jurisdiction refuse such an application, the applicant may make an application for the same purpose to Quarter Sessions, either by letter addressed to the clerk of the peace or in person to the court.

Section 3 lays a duty on the clerk to the justices (the formalities being completed) to transmit to the clerk of the peace the notice of appeal and the recognizance, if any, together with a statement of the decision from which the appeal is brought and the last known or usual place of abode of the parties to the appeal. The conviction must be drawn up in the form prescribed in rule 19 of the Magistrates' Courts Rules, 1952. The clerk of the peace then enters the appeal and in due course gives notice to the appellant, to the other party to the appeal, and to the clerk to the justices, of the date, time and place for the hearing of the appeal.

It is good notice if sent by post in a registered letter addressed to the last or usual place of abode or by recorded delivery.

Section 85 of the Magistrates' Courts Act, 1952, lays down that an appellant may abandon an appeal to Quarter Sessions not later than the third day before the day fixed for hearing the appeal by giving notice in writing to the clerk to the court of summary jurisdiction against whose decision the appeal is brought. On receipt of such notice the clerk to the justices shall forthwith give notice of abandonment to the other party and to the clerk of the peace. Once an appeal has been abandoned, the appellant cannot go back on his decision, and the clerk of the peace has no further jurisdiction in the matter.

A person who is convicted at a magistrates' court has also a right to apply to the convicting justices, on the ground that the conviction is wrong in law or is in excess of jurisdiction, to state a case for the opinion of the High Court on the question of law or jurisdiction involved. Once, however, he has made such an application, his right of appeal to Quarter Sessions shall cease (section 87 (4) Magistrates' Courts Act, 1952).

By section 11 of the Quarter Sessions Act, 1849 (Baines Act), it was enacted that on an appeal to Quarter Sessions the parties may, at any time after the notice of appeal, consent to a special case being drawn under the order of a judge of the High Court and submitted to the High Court for its decision.

The judgment of the High Court may then be entered on motion by either party at the Sessions next or next but one after it is given, and is of the same effect as if it had been given by the court of Quarter Sessions upon an appeal duly entered and continued.

On receipt of the papers in connection with an appeal to Quarter Sessions, the clerk of the peace will assure himself that all is in order and, in this connection, he may find that the notice of appeal was given outside the statutory 14 days. In such a case he should enter the appeal, and give the statutory notices regarding the date of hearing, and when the appeal is called on for hearing he should point out to the chairman that the appeal is out of time. Section 84 of the Magistrates' Courts Act, 1952, enables a chairman of quarter sessions, at his discretion, to allow the omission to be rectified by written notice being given in court.

Trial by Jury — Quarter Sessions

Prior to the coming into force of the Criminal Justice Act, 1948, re-enacted in the Magistrates' Courts Act, 1952, failure to give notice of appeal within the 14 day period acted as a complete estoppel and the hands of Quarter Sessions were completely tied. Now, however, under the provisions of section 84 of the Act any person who wishes to appeal outside the prescribed period of 14 days may apply in writing to the clerk of the peace, and the court of Quarter Sessions may, if it thinks fit, direct that a notice of appeal previously given by the applicant after the expiration of the statutory period, or any such notice given by him within such further time as may be specified in the direction, shall be treated as if given within the said period.

The powers of Quarter Sessions in relation to such applications are exercised by the chairman or deputy chairman. Since the coming into force of this provision many such applications have been successfully made to Quarter Sessions, and the defect may even be remedied on the date of the hearing.

As has already been pointed out in Chapter 2, the normal dates for the hearing of appeals at Quarter Sessions are fixed annually, and it is the duty of the clerk of the peace to enter appeals as they are received by him for hearing at the next practicable date. In this connection it must be borne in mind that reasonable notice of the date of hearing has to be given; as a general rule, seven clear days' notice is given. The provisions of the Betting Act, 1960, laid down this period as a statutory minimum for appeals in connection with that Act.

Since, however, notices of appeal are frequently received by the clerk of the peace less than 7 days from the appointed date for hearing appeals, and as some of these appeals relate to persons who are in custody, actually serving sentences against which they desire to appeal, it is unavoidable that such appeals have to be entered for hearing within that period. It would not be fair to postpone the appeals of such appellants until the next normal appeal day, which could well be some three or four weeks ahead. It could even happen in such a case that a short sentence might have been served before the appeal could be heard.

Where the appellant has been granted bail pending appeal, the matter can fairly be left to be dealt with on the normal date. Since the abolition of the appeal committee the chairman can always direct the clerk of the peace to enter an appeal at any time should the occasion necessitate it. The same principle applies to appellants in respect of motoring offences in which the penalty has included a period of disqualification from holding a driving licence. Since, here again, magistrates' courts have power to suspend any disqualification pending an appeal (see section 105 of the Road Traffic Act, 1960) where this power has been exercised, there is not the same urgency for the determining of the appeal as will justify the giving of less than the usual 7 days' notice.

Having given due notice of the date or dates of hearing, the clerk of the peace has to complete a list of cases for hearing on each of the days in question. The method of allocation to the various courts that are sitting is a matter for each individual clerk of the peace. The notice will, however, contain only the following information: name of appellant, name of respondent and particulars of appeal.

By a recent direction of the Divisional Court, clerks of the peace have been instructed not to allow chairmen of quarter sessions to have access to the notes of evidence taken by the clerks to the justices, the only papers which should be handed to the chairman being a copy of the notice of appeal together with a copy of the conviction at the magistrates' court. This direction was, however, qualified to the effect that a chairman of quarter sessions may look at the notes of evidence to help him with regard to the probable length of the case or to see if any point of law is likely to arise.

An appeal at Quarter Sessions against a conviction is a rehearing, and either the appellant or respondent may without notice call witnesses before Quarter Sessions who were not called before the magistrates. The notes made by the clerk to the justices are only notes and are in no way comparable with the depositions which are taken prior to a committal to Quarter Sessions on indictment. An occasion may occur during the course of the hearing of the appeal when some point arises relative to the notes taken by the clerk to the justices, in which event, the consent of both parties having been given, the clerk of the peace may hand a copy to the chairman.

As can be imagined, a considerable variety of appeals come up for hearing before Quarter Sessions. Of recent years the number of appeals relating to motoring offences has tended to increase year by year. Since the coming into force of the Betting and Gaming Act, 1960 (now virtually replaced by the Betting, Gaming and Lotteries Act, 1963), Quarter Sessions have had to deal with a large number of appeals in respect of refusals by licensing committees of the various petty sessional divisions to allow either bookmakers' permits in respect of individuals or betting office permits in respect of premises.

Quarter Sessions formerly used to hear appeals against rating assessments, but that jurisdiction was taken away from them in 1948 by the Local Government Act, 1948. At one time quite a number of highway applications were dealt with at Sessions, but by the Highways Act, 1959, an alternative method of closing or diverting highways was enacted, and nowadays all that Quarter Sessions has to do is duly to enrol the said closures or diversions.

Licensing

The Licensing Act, 1953, which has itself been extensively amended by the Licensing Act, 1961, was enacted with a view to consolidating earlier enactments dealing with justices' licences for the sale by retail of intoxicating liquor and the registration of clubs.

Section 2 (2) of the Licensing Act, 1953, enacted that "For a county licensing district the licensing justices shall be a committee of the justices acting for the petty sessions area forming the district known as the 'divisional licensing committee'."

Prior to the coming into force of section 12 of the Licensing Act, 1961, licences granted by justices in connection with the sale of liquor required confirmation by the Licensing Committee of Quarter Sessions which used to meet annually for this purpose.

Section 12, however, introduced a new procedure in connection with the grant of justices' licences, and enacted that "No justices' licence granted after the coming into force of this section shall require confirmation". It also introduced a new right of appeal to Quarter Sessions in the following words: "there shall be an appeal to quarter sessions against any decision of licensing justices granting or refusing to grant a new justices licence, or an ordinary removal of a justices' licence, and against any decision of licensing justices as to the condition of a justices' on-licence".

The result is that, whereas for many years after the coming into force of the Licensing Act, 1910, Quarter Sessions annually appointed a County Licensing Committee to deal with confirmations and compensation, many of the licences thus referred to Quarter Sessions were unopposed and the proceedings at that court became, over the years often, virtually a formality. Opposed licences used to take up much more of the courts' time, most of the opposition coming from the trade.

Then in 1953 by the Licensing Act of that year the title of the committee was changed to that of the County Confirming and Compensation Committee. The number of confirmations for the consideration of Quarter Sessions continued to decrease year by year until the Licensing Act, 1961, delivered the final death knell to Quarter Sessions as regards their jurisdiction in respect of the confirmation of justices' licences. Once more the name of the committee was altered, on this occasion the title being abridged to that of County Compensation Committee. The year 1962 was, therefore, the last occasion in which county confirming and compensation committees were destined to meet for the purpose of carrying out this portion of their duties.

The Licensing Act, 1953, enacts that the compensation authority for a county licensing district shall be the County Compensation Committee (see section 18 (1) (a) of the Licensing Act, 1953). This committee is appointed in accordance with the approval of the Secretary of State, and the number and quorum of the committee shall be such as shall be so determined.

The compensation fund consists of contributions provided by the trade itself, and if a licence is extinguished, the compensation is provided out of the county compensation fund. A compensation authority, when considering compensation for an extinguished licence, is required to hold three meetings — a preliminary meeting, a principal meeting and a supplemental meeting. The preliminary meeting must be held before the last day in May.

References to the Compensation Committee have become very rare. The clerk of the peace, who is usually the clerk to the Compensating Committee; has a duty to convene a meeting of the committee at such times as shall be necessary or expedient for the purposes of the Licensing Acts.

Since the committee has to report its proceedings to the court of Quarter Sessions at the Epiphany Quarter Sessions each year, the clerk of the peace may consider it necessary to hold a formal meeting once a year for this purpose. In the meantime the compensation fund builds up. This fund is used for the purpose of paying compensation in the event of a licence being extinguished. One of the reasons for holding an annual meeting of the Compensation Committee is to decide whether a levy should be imposed with a view to building up this fund.

CHAPTER 5

After-trial duties — Appeals to Court of Criminal Appeal

Committal warrants — Estreat roll — Return to Treasury of fines — After-trial calendar — Notices to clerks to justices — Witness and juror expenses — Costs in criminal cases — Legal aid certificates — Examination of bills of costs — Appeals to Court of Criminal Appeal — Appeals to the House of Lords

THE trial being completed and the sentence of the court having been pronounced by the judge or chairman, we can now turn to some of the after-trial duties which fall on a clerk of assizes or a clerk of the peace, in order that the sentence of the court may be duly implemented. Before, however, proceeding to deal specifically with these duties, it is relevant to point out here that section 3 (1) of the Administration of Justice (Miscellaneous Provisions) Act, 1938, reference to which has been made in connection with the title "adjournments", provides that, if after a date has been fixed for an adjourned sessions, and the sessions when held are not concluded before the next date fixed for the general or Quarter Sessions of the peace, any proceedings which might have been dealt with at the adjourned sessions may be dealt with at the later sessions and any recognizances are automatically enlarged.

The effect of the above provision is that the defendant's bail and witnesses' recognizances relevant to any trials that have not been reached are automatically enlarged without the necessity of a formal application having to be made to the court. Where, however, the trial of any defendant who is in custody does not

After-trial duties — Appeals to Court of Criminal Appeal 105

take place — and the reason for this is quite often at the defendant's own request — it is necessary for the clerk of the peace to have such a defendant brought into court in order that the chairman can inform him that his trial will be postponed until the next sessions. The importance of this is that committal warrants have to be issued for the purpose of committing such a defendant to the next sessions; without a further warrant, the prison governor would have no authority to hold such a person beyond the last day of the sessions to which he had originally been committed for trial.

COMMITTAL WARRANTS

The most vital document that has to be seen to immediately after a trial is over and a sentence of imprisonment has resulted therefrom is the committal warrant. This document, which has to be signed by the clerk of the court, is the authority, as we have already seen, for the governor of the prison or other institution to which the court has sentenced the defendant to be taken to receive the said defendant into custody. Without a warrant no governor can receive or hold any person, or he may find himself the subject of habeas corpus proceedings. Great care, therefore, must be taken to ensure that the committal warrant sets out the true judgment of the court; and since the indictment is the official record of the court proceedings, it is on the entry made by the clerk of the count on the indictment that the committal warrant is based. The warrant must indicate clearly whether the judgment of the court is concurrent or consecutive as regards the several counts, in the event of the prisoner having been found guilty on more than one count in an indictment.

In the event of judgment having been respited for the purpose of obtaining a mental or medical report on the prisoner, this fact should be stated on the committal warrant.

There are three main forms of committal warrants, the first is known as commitment — general form, and includes:

(a) Imprisonment for the space of . . .
(b) Detention in corrective training for a period of . . .
(c) Remand in custody until . . . and be then brought up to take his trial/receive judgment.
(d) Detention in a Borstal institution.
(e) Detention in preventive detention.
(f) Detention in a detention centre.

The second is also known as commitment — general form, and includes the same headings as above, but is applicable in relation to persons who have been convicted before a magistrates' court and committed to Quarter Sessions for sentence.

The third form applies to appellants who appeal to Quarter Sessions against sentences imposed on them by magistrates' courts, and is therefore somewhat different in its wording and runs as follows:

> Whereas A.B. (hereinafter called the appellant) was, on the . . . . . . day of. . . . . 19. . . . convicted of . . . by the Court of Summary Jurisdiction sitting at . . . in the said county. And IT WAS ADJUDGED that the appellant be . . .
> AND WHEREAS the appellant gave notice of his intention to appeal against the said (convictions) (sentences)
> NOW the said appeal having been heard it is ordered that the said (convictions) (sentences) (be) (be varied) and that the appellant be committed into the custody of the (Keeper of one of Her Majesty's Prisons) (Warden of H.M. Detention Centre) at . . . there to undergo the sentence(s) adjudged by (the said Court of Summary Jurisdiction) (this Court), less those days already served by the said appellant.
> By the Court

With regard to appeals to Quarter Sessions by persons who have been sentenced at a magistrates' court, it will be noted that an appellant is automatically entitled to a remission on his sentence in respect of such days as he had already served prior to the hearing of his appeal. There is, therefore, no need for the court to make any pronouncement on this when dismissing an appeal.

Approved school orders have also to be made out when a

young person between the ages of 14 and 17 has been sentenced to detention in an approved school.

Sections 8 and 9 of the Childrens Act, 1963, which came into force on the 1st February 1964, introduced a new method of drawing up these orders.

Section 8 enacts that the school to which a person is to be sent in pursuance of an approved school order shall not be specified in the order, the order being the authority for his detention, and the choice of school is to be made by the Secretary of State. There is also provision for a parent or nearest adult relative to apply to a juvenile court within 30 days of a person's arrival at an approved school for a declaration of religious persuasion.

Section 9 enacts that every approved school order shall take effect immediately, and provides places to which a person may be committed in custody before he can be sent to an approved school, i.e. (*a*) if the approved school order is made on a conviction or finding of guilt — any place to which he might have been committed on remand, and (*b*) in any other case, any place of safety.

Provision is also made for a juvenile court in respect of a person who has attained 14, if they are satisfied that he is of so unruly a character, to treat the remand centre as a place of safety. If, therefore, a juvenile court is satisfied regarding a person who has attained the age of 14, that he is of so unruly a character that he cannot safely be detained in a remand home or other place of safety or is of so depraved a character that he is not fit to be so detained, the remand centre may be treated as a place of safety.

Other court orders which have to be signed are probation orders. Before signing these orders the clerk must satisfy himself that the orders are in fact drawn up in accordance with the court's directions. Normally this presents no difficulty, since the majority of such orders are in a set form. Sometimes, however, the court may decide to add special terms to the normal ones, and these have to be carefully noted. One thing a court cannot do is to insert a condition making the regular payments of monies a condition of a probation order, and a court has always to bear in mind that any condition should be of such a nature that it is reasonably possible for the probationer to carry out the requirement in question.

There are also recognizances to be drawn up and signed, in cases where persons have been bound over to keep the peace and to come up for judgment if called on. These orders, if imposed by Quarter Sessions, have to be signed by the person so bound over, any surety or sureties, two justices, and the clerk of the peace.

Before finally leaving the question of committal warrants, it is as well perhaps to refer to one more aspect regarding the powers of Assizes and Quarter Sessions with regard to sentencing. The normal practice is for a sentence imposed by these courts to take effect from the beginning of the day on which it is imposed, unless the court otherwise directs (see section 17(1) Criminal Justice Act, 1962, as regards Assize Courts, and section 12, Stipendiary Magistrates' Act, 1858, in relation to Quarter Sessions). A sentence cannot be ante-dated so as to run from an earlier date than the first day of the Assizes or Sessions during which it is passed. Reference has already been made in the previous chapter to the powers of these courts in regard to the sentencing of a person who is the subject of a previous sentence for an earlier conviction, and also to the importance of it being clearly pronounced whether sentences are to be concurrent or consecutive.

The effect of the above is to allow a person who is sentenced to one day's imprisonment to be discharged forthwith, or indeed, if a prisoner has been in custody before trial, a sentence of imprisonment for that period of time must in consequence of the provisions of section 17 (2) of the Criminal Justice Act, 1962, result in the immediate discharge of the prisoner, unless he is serving a sentence in respect of another offence.

With regard to appeals to Quarter Sessions by persons who have been sentenced at a magistrates' court it will be noted that

After-trial duties — Appeals to Court of Criminal Appeal

an appellant is automatically entitled to a remission on his sentence in respect of such days as he has already served prior to the hearing of his appeal. There is, therefore, no need for the court to make any pronouncement on this when dismissing an appeal.

ESTREAT ROLL — RETURN TO TREASURY OF FINES

It is convenient to deal jointly with the above two headings since they are so closely interlinked. The powers of courts of Assize and Quarter Sessions with regard to fines imposed and estreated recognizances are regulated by sections 14 and 15 of the Criminal Justice Act, 1948, by virtue of which they are empowered to (*a*) allow time for the payment of the amount of a fine or forfeited recognizance, (*b*) direct payment by instalments, (*c*) fix a term of imprisonment in default of payment of the fine or forfeited recognizance, and (*d*) in the case of a recognizance, discharge the recognizance or reduce the amount due thereunder. Any imprisonment fixed in default of payment of a fine shall not exceed 12 months, and may be ordered to run consecutively to any other term of imprisonment either imposed by the court or to which the person in question is already subject.

Thus where a defendant has failed to surrender to his bail, and finally stands his trial as a result of being brought before the court through the medium of a certificate of indictment preferred and signed or a bench warrant, section 14 further empowers a court of Assize or Quarter Sessions, where both the maximum sentence of imprisonment and a fine have been imposed for an offence, to impose a further sentence for imprisonment in default of payment, such sentence being ordered to run consecutively to the first mentioned term of imprisonment, but no such term shall exceed 12 months.

It is worthy of note in passing, that, prior to the coming into force of the Criminal Justice Act, 1948, courts of Assize and Quarter Sessions had no power to impose a fine for felony, though for misdemeanor they could always do so. Under the old procedure persons so fined could be ordered to be detained in custody until the fine was paid. Section 14 of the Criminal Justice Act, 1948, however, introduced a new procedure. It is necessary for the court, however, to remember that if time is given for payment of a fine, an alternative term of imprisonment must be pronounced at the same time. If this is not done, the sheriff will not be able to enforce the estreat, and the defendant will escape without having to pay the fine.

A further provision of the above section 14 is that where a fine is imposed, or recognizance estreated, by or before a court of Assize or Quarter Sessions, the court is empowered to amend any previous order made by it with regard to (*a*) further time to pay a fine or estreated recognizance, or (*b*) instalments, upon application being made in writing, in the case of the Central Criminal Court to the clerk of the court; or regarding any other court of Assize to the clerk of assize, and in the case of a court of Quarter Sessions to the clerk of the peace. The application is dealt with at the Central Criminal Court by a judge of that court; at any other Assize court by a judge of the High Court; and at Quarter Sessions by the chairman or any deputy chairman of that court.

Payment of a part of the fine or amount due under a recognizance will have the effect of reducing the total number of days' imprisonment proportionately.

The method of recovery of fines and estreated recognizances in courts of Assize, the Central Criminal Court and the Crown courts is prescribed by section 32 of the Queen's Remembrancer Act, 1859, which enacts that the clerk of assize or clerk of the court must within 14 days of the imposition of a fine or the forfeiture of recognizances, copy on a roll all such fines and estreated recognizances and send a copy of such roll with a writ of execution to the sheriff.

At Quarter Sessions the recovery of fines etc. is regulated by the Levy of Fines Acts, 1822 and 1823, which enact that the clerk of the peace must copy on a roll all fines and recognizances estreated at a session and within 21 days after the adjournment of the session send a copy of the roll with a writ of distringas and capias or of fieri facias and capias to the sheriff of the county for execution. This estreat roll and writ constitutes the authority to the sheriff for proceeding to the immediate levying and recovery of such fines, etc.

It is of interest here to note the wording of the writ which accompanies the estreat roll when it is sent to the sheriff — it runs as follows:

> ELIZABETH II by the Grace of God of the United Kingdom of Great Britain and Northern Ireland and of her other Realms and Territories Queen, Head of the Commonwealth, Defender of the Faith, to the Sheriff for the County of . . .
>
> Greeting. You are hereby required and commanded, as you regard yourself and all yours, that you omit not by reason of any Liberty in your County, but that you enter the same, and of all the Goods and Chattels of all and singular the Persons in the Roll to this Writ annexed, you cause to be Levied all and singular the Debts and sums of money upon them in the same Roll severally charged, so that the Money may be ready for payment at the next General or Quarter Session of the Peace, to be paid over in such manner as the Commissioners of Her Majesty's Treasury may direct, and if any of the several Debts cannot be levied, by reason of no Goods or Chattels being to be found belonging to the Parties, then in all cases that you take the Bodies of the Parties refusing to pay the aforesaid Debts and lodge them in the Gaol of the County, there to remain until they pay the same, or be discharged by the authority of the said Commissioners, or otherwise in due course of Law.
>
> Dated the........day of........in the........Year of our Reign
> Clerk of the Peace for the County of . . .

The sheriff must at the next ensuing session return the writ and roll and state on the back of the roll what has been done in the execution of the process. A further duty is laid on the clerk of the peace to return to the Treasury a copy of the sheriff's return to the writs within 20 days (see section 5, Levy of Fines Act, 1823).

The sheriff's duty is to execute all process with regard to the recovery of these sums.

AFTER-TRIAL CALENDAR

Another of the duties that fall on the clerk of the court after the final adjournment of an Assizes or Sessions is the making up of the after-trial calendar. This speaks for itself, and is in effect a complete record of all the trials (whether pleas of guilty or not guilty), breaches of probation and other orders and respited judgments and, in the case of Quarter Sessions, sentences in respect of persons who have been committed to them for sentence, that have taken place in all the courts that have been dealing with the cases in the calendar of the Assizes or Sessions that has just ended.

The after-trial calendar is really a corrected version of the pre-trial calendar with, of course, the additional information now available in order to allow the filling in of the three final items which appear in relation to each prisoner, namely: Tried before . . .; Verdict or plea . . .; Sentence or order of the court . . . The clerk of the court, having amended the pre-trial calendar so as to conform with the results of the completed session, will send a copy to the prison governor for him to have it printed, this being a matter for the prison governor and not for the clerk of the court. When finally completed, the after-trial calendar is sent to the Home Office, prison authorities and to New Scotland Yard for official record purposes. The Criminal Record Office then check any queries that may arise with the clerk of the court. When it is settled, the after-trial calendar is then signed by the prison governor and by the clerk of the court, assize or peace, as the case may be.

NOTICES TO CLERKS TO JUSTICES

A further duty which falls on clerks of the peace only, relates to the notification of the results of appeals. Section 1 of the Summary Jurisdiction (Appeals) Act, 1933, which replaced section 31 of the Summary Jurisdiction Act, 1879, and has itself been amended by the 9th Schedule of the Criminal Justice Act,

After-trial duties — Appeals to Court of Criminal Appeal 113

1948, and the 6th Schedule of the Magistrates' Courts Act, 1952, lays a duty on the clerk of the peace to send to the clerk to the court by whom the decision appealed against was given, for entry in his register, a memorandum of the decision of Quarter Sessions, and if the appeal was an appeal against a conviction or sentence or against an order, to enclose a like memorandum on the conviction or order, as the case may be. Whenever any copy or certificate of the conviction or order is made, a copy of the memorandum shall be added thereto and shall be sufficient evidence of the conviction or order. So much for appeals to Quarter Sessions. It is also the practice in some courts to notify the magistrates' courts of the results of all cases that have been respectively committed to them for trial and or sentence.

WITNESS AND JUROR EXPENSES

It is proposed now to deal with the payments which are required to be made whilst a court of assize or sessions is actually in session. These payments concern jurors' and witnesses' expenses. This aspect of the matter as regards jurors has already been fully referred to in Chapter 3, and it is therefore unnecessary to make more than a passing reference to it in the present chapter. From time to time individual jurors desire to be released from further jury service during the course of the session, and are paid their expenses when so released. The majority of jurors, however, are paid after they have completed the final trial for which their attendance is required at any particular sessions.

With regard to witnesses, the costs which can be ordered to be paid are regulated by the Witnesses' Allowances Regulations, 1955, as amended by the Witnesses' Allowances Regulations, 1958, the Witnesses' Allowances Regulations, 1960, and the Witnesses' Allowances Regulations, 1966 (see p. 138).

The allowance in respect of a professional witness (doctor, barrister, dentist, etc.) for attending to give professional evidence is not to exceed 8 guineas a day, or if the witness is absent from his place of residence or practice for less than 4 hours, 4 guineas. If, however, he incurs expenses by providing a locum in his absence, this amount can be exceeded.

There are two points of importance to note here: first, that the witness must give professional evidence, and, secondly, that if the same witness in fact gives evidence at the same court on the same day in more than one case, then the allowance to which he is entitled remains at the maximum of 8 guineas.

Expert witnesses may be allowed such amount as the court may consider reasonable having regard to the nature and difficulty of the work necessarily involved. There are occasions on which the court has to determine whether a witness qualifies to be paid on the basis of having given his evidence by way of an expert or merely as a professional in his particular occupation.

Witnesses (other than expert or professional) who lose remuneration or necessarily incur expense, which would not otherwise have been incurred, are entitled to an allowance not exceeding 50*s.* a day in respect of such loss or 25*s.* if his absence from work does not exceed 4 hours.

A witness (other than professional or expert) shall be allowed a subsistence allowance not exceeding: for less than 4 hours 5*s.* a day, for 4–8 hours 10*s.* a day and in excess of 8 hours 12*s.* 6*d.* a day (see also p. 138).

Travelling expenses are allowed as follows:

(1) Second-class fare for travel by railway or other public conveyance.
(2) Travel by a hired vehicle — the sum actually paid for the hire or an allowance at 1*s.* 6*d.* a mile, whichever be the less.
(3) Private conveyance — if the court is satisfied that it is reasonable to so travel — $7\frac{1}{2}d.$ a mile each way.
(4) In any other case 3*d.* a mile.

The court is also empowered to make extra allowances for the conveyance to and from court of witnesses suffering from serious illness, and also for the carriage of heavy exhibits.

Such fees are allowed for an interpreter as the court shall consider reasonable. Certain courts have of recent years agreed to pay interpreters a fee of 4 guineas for a period not exceeding 4 hours including travelling, or 8 guineas for a period not exceeding 8 hours including travelling. This fee being payable both at a magistrates court or at Quarter Sessions. An interpreter, however, does not receive a subsistence allowance, but in addition is paid travelling expenses.

No witness allowance is allowed in respect of a member of the police force attending court in his capacity as such, or a whole time prison officer, or for a prisoner produced in custody.

A witness is defined as meaning a person properly attending court to give evidence, whether or not he gives evidence. There is also provision for the payment of allowance in respect of witnesses who are necessarily absent from their place of residence overnight to attend as a witness, the 1960 regulations having raised the sum so allowed from 27s. to 40s.

The clerk of the court has a duty to check the allowances claimed by witnesses. He must satisfy himself, for instance, that a professional witness did in fact give his evidence in that capacity, and did not merely speak as a witness to character. The clerk of the court is dependent on the information being given to him correctly by the witness who, unlike a juror, does not have to fill in a form himself. Difficulties have arisen regarding the payment of witnesses for an appellant or respondent in an appeal to Quarter Sessions. Neither the Costs in Criminal Cases Act, 1952, or the Summary Jurisdiction (Appeals) Act, 1933, make any specific provision for such payments.

In the case of a person who has been granted an appeal aid certificate this difficulty has been got over by authorizing solicitors' out-of-pocket expenses under rule 1 (3) of the Appeal Aid Certificate Rules, 1960, to include such payments, but in a case where no such certificate has been granted, witnesses' allowances cannot be paid except in an appeal against a conviction under section 4 of the Vagrancy Act, 1824.

COSTS IN CRIMINAL CASES

All orders with regard to costs made by a court of assize or quarter sessions have to be drawn up by the clerk of the court and signed by him. These orders may take the form of orders made on defendants who have been convicted on indictment, and ordered to pay a sum of money towards the costs of the prosecution: or of orders made in favour of a defendant who has been allowed costs on his acquittal by a jury. Section 1 of the Costs in Criminal Cases Act, 1952 (which repealed section 44 of the Criminal Justice Act, 1948), empowers a court of assize or quarter sessions before which any person is prosecuted, or tried, to order payment out of local funds, if the accused is acquitted, of the costs of the defence. Subsection (2) defines such costs as "the expenses properly incurred by him in carrying on his defence".

It is proposed now, therefore, to deal more fully with this important financial aspect of the duties of a clerk of assize or of the peace. Speaking generally, the clerk is responsible for making out the court orders relative to the payment of costs in respect of cases tried at Assizes or Quarter Sessions. A clerk of the peace is also responsible for the supervision of costs allowed in cases tried before the magistrates.

The costs awarded by Assizes or Quarter Sessions ordered to be paid out of local funds in respect of criminal cases are now regulated by the provisions of the Costs in Criminal Cases Act, 1952, which is described as "an Act to consolidate certain enactments relating to costs in criminal cases with corrections and improvements made under the Consolidation of (Procedure) Act, 1949". This Act repealed the Costs in Criminal Cases Act, 1908, which had previously controlled the procedure in this matter, and came into force on the 1st January 1953.

After-trial duties — Appeals to Court of Criminal Appeal

The provisions of this Act are so important that it is as well to bear in mind a short summary of the main features contained therein, in so far as they affect both Assize courts and Quarter Sessions. Section 1 deals generally with the payment out of local funds of costs awarded by an Assize court or Quarter Sessions to the prosecution or to an accused person who has been acquitted on indictment. Section 2 deals with costs awarded by Assizes or Quarter Sessions as between parties, and section 6 covers similar costs awarded at the magistrates' court. This section also contains the following provision: "that in cases where the magistrates have determined not to commit an accused person for trial and they order the prosecution to pay the whole or part of the costs of the defence if the amount exceeds £25 the prosecution may appeal to Quarter Sessions."

Section 7 defines local funds in cases committed in an administrative county as being the county fund.

Sections 8–11 deal with the method of payment of costs ordered to be paid out of local funds by Assize courts, Quarter Sessions or by the magistrates' court, section 11 enacting that "The Treasurer of a county on whom an order is made for a payment of any sum on account of costs under this Act shall, upon sight of the order, pay out of the county fund to the person named in the order, or his duly authorized agent, the sum specified in the order."

Section 12 empowers the Secretary of State to make regulations generally for carrying the Act into effect and in particular in regard to:

(*a*) the rates or scales of payment;
(*b*) the manner in which an officer of the court making a payment to any person in respect of his attendance to give evidence is to be repaid out of local funds; and
(*c*) the form of orders, certificates and notices under this Act.

Section 14, as amended by the Criminal Justice Administration

Act, 1962, applies the provisions of the Act to persons committed to Quarter Sessions under section 28 and 29 of the Magistrates' Courts Act, 1952, to incorrigible rogues so committed, and to appeals under the Vagrancy Act, 1824. Otherwise the Act does not apply to appeals heard by Quarter Sessions. Section 17 defines counsel's or solicitors' fees as coming within the provisions of the Act.

The certificates relating to cases dealt with at the magistrates' court are sent to the clerk of the peace, who after examining them lays them before the next court of Quarter Sessions for approval. These certificates also include the statutory payments due to clerks to the justices in respect of indictable cases tried summarily.

The certificates relating to cases committed for trial come up for review when the clerk of assize or the clerk of the peace, acting in his capacity as taxing officer on behalf of the court, is considering the fees that should be allowed to prosecuting solicitors and counsel. The principles which are applied are the same, whether the prosecutor is the Director of Public Prosecutions, the Commissioner of Police or a public body such as the Board of Trade or Inland Revenue or a private prosecutor.

The general principle that has to be borne in mind is, as laid down in section 1 (2) of the costs in Criminal Cases Act, 1952, that the amounts should be such sums as appear to the court reasonably sufficient to compensate the prosecutor (or accused) for the expenses properly incurred by him.

Section 18 of the Criminal Justice Act, 1962, makes provision for the recovery of costs incurred by any court of Assize or court of Quarter Sessions, where a person has been there tried, sentenced or dealt with under the provisions which give powers to petty sessional courts to commit to sessions other than those for which they act. The Court Expenses (Recovery) Regulations, 1963, which came into operation in April 1963, set out the method by which the sum to be recoverable by one local authority from another is to be ascertained. The purpose underlying this form of committal is to assure, wherever it is possible, that no person who is committed for trial will have to wait longer than a maximum period of 8 weeks before standing his trial.

LEGAL AID CERTIFICATES

It is now proposed to deal with the subject of free legal aid in so far as this affects Assize courts and Quarter Sessions. All such courts have to determine what fees are payable to solicitors and counsel in connection with their services resulting from the granting of legal aid certificates. The Poor Prisoners Defence Act, 1930, enacted that

> Any person committed for trial for an indictable offence shall be entitled to free legal aid in the preparation and conduct of his defence at the trial and to have solicitor and counsel assigned to him for that purpose in the prescribed manner, if a certificate (defence certificate), is granted in respect of him in accordance with the provisions of the Act.

Such certificates can be granted (a) by the committing justices at the time of his committal, or (b) by the judge or chairman of the court before which he is to be tried.

No defence certificate shall be granted to a person unless it appears to the committing magistrates or the judge or chairman that his means are insufficient to enable him to obtain legal representation. If the court is satisfied as to any person's lack of means, and that the circumstances (including the nature of the defence, if any) make it desirable in the interests of justice that the defendant should be legally represented, the certificate should be granted. The tendency of recent years has been for the courts to allow many more legal aid certificates than was formally the case, Lord Parker (the Lord Chief Justice) having expressed a strong view in favour of this practice.

Another factor which used to have to be taken into account was the gravity of the charge or any exceptional circumstances: this, however, has no longer been applicable since the 1st April 1963, when the provisions of section 18 (2) of the Legal Aid and Advice Act, 1949, came into operation. Section 4 of the Poor

Prisoners' Defence Act, 1930, empowered the Attorney-General with the approval of the Lord Chancellor and a Secretary of State, to make rules for carrying the Act into effect, and a series of such rules has in fact been established.

By virtue of the provisions of the Poor Prisoners (Counsel and Solicitor) Rules, 1931, every clerk of assize and clerk of the peace has to keep a list of solicitors who are willing to undertake the defence of poor prisoners. Copies of this list have to be circulated from time to time to all the clerks to the justices in the county.

A similar list of the names of counsel who are willing to undertake such defences has to be kept by every clerk of assize and clerk of the peace and circulated to the clerks of the justices.*
Both lists have to be kept up to date by additions and deletions as and when notified to the clerks of assize or clerks of the peace.

This section also lays a further duty on clerks of assize, clerks of the peace and clerks to justices to make a return of all cases in which applications for defence certificates are made, whether they be granted or not, to the Secretary of State for the Home Department at such times as he may direct.

A duty is placed on clerks to justices to forward to the clerk of assize or the clerk of the peace defence certificates, together with the name of the solicitor assigned, as soon as they are granted. On receipt of the defence certificate the clerk of assize or the clerk of the peace has to supply a copy of the depositions to the solicitor assigned.

Section 18 (3) of the Legal Aid and Advice Act, 1949, which came into force on the 1st April 1952, lays down that before a person is granted free legal aid he may be required to furnish a written statement in the prescribed form about matters relevant for determining whether his means are insufficient to enable him to obtain legal aid.

Whilst on the subject of legal aid certificates, it is convenient to refer to the practice in relation to appeals by appellants to

*This obligation as regards counsel is no longer operative (see Appendix I, p. 138).

After-trial duties — Appeals to Court of Criminal Appeal

Quarter Sessions in respect of convictions or sentences before magistrates. In such cases the procedure is laid down in section 2 (1) of the Summary Jurisdiction (Appeals) Act, 1933. The application has to be made by letter addressed to the clerk to the justices. If such an application is refused, subsection (3) enables a person to make a further application to Quarter Sessions. An appellant who has neither applied by letter to the clerk to the justices nor applied to Quarter Sessions, is entitled to make his application in person to Quarter Sessions on the date fixed for the hearing of his appeal.

A similar right attaches to any defendant on his appearance to stand his trial at Assizes or Quarter Sessions, when the judge or chairman can request counsel to undertake his defence. Such grants of legal aid are limited to counsel only; should it transpire, however, that a defendant requires the presence of witnesses at his trial, the judge or chairman will in all probability adjourn the hearing and grant a defence certificate which covers both solicitor and counsel.

There is also the right of any occupant of the dock to ask for a "dock brief". By long-established custom he is then entitled to choose any counsel robed in court (other than the prosecuting counsel in the case or any Queen's Counsel who may be in court) to appear for him. In such cases the prisoner has himself to produce the fee of £2 4s. 6d.

The origin of a "dock brief" is somewhat obscure, but it is certainly of earlier origin than 1900. This is one of the exceptional cases when a barrister may be instructed directly by his client without the intervention of a solicitor. The fee should be handed to counsel as an essential preliminary before he undertakes the dock defence. Originally the fee was £1 3s. 6d. In October 1951, however, the General Council of the Bar resolved that the minimum fee which up to that time had been payable to counsel and which had remained at £1 1s. 0d. since before 1888, should be raised to £2 2s. 0d except where statute otherwise provided. And it was also further resolved that the new minimum fee of £2 4s. 6d. should extend to dock briefs, the extra half-crown being the barristers' clerks fee.

An order has to be drawn up by the court in respect of every defence certificate. This takes the form of a direction to the County Treasurer to pay the sum approved by the court out of local funds, such sum to include fees of solicitor and counsel, costs of copy depositions and any other expenses properly incurred. Section 23 of the Legal Aid and Advice Act, 1949, lays down that the ultimate liability is to be transferred from local to general funds, except in respect of the sums which are payable under the Costs in Criminal Cases Act, 1952. The payments are made out of local funds initially and recovered from the Treasury later. Section 18 (4) of the above Act, which came into operation on the 1st April 1963, extends the provisions of the Poor Prisoners' Defence Act, 1930, to cover persons committed to Quarter Sessions as rogues and vagabonds under the Vagrancy Act, 1824, and persons committed for sentence. This section further extended the right to legal aid to cover proceedings in relation to the sentence or order to be passed on a defendant; in other words, to cover respited judgments. Good use has been made of this extension in cases which are affected by the provisions of the Commonwealth Immigrants Act, 1962, and it is now an established rule that where such notices are served the defendant should be granted legal aid.

Incidentally, this particular statute (Legal Aid and Advice Act 1949) is a good example of what was referred to in the introductory remarks concerning piecemeal legislation (see p. xvii).

The form which an applicant for free legal aid has to fill in and sign is worthy of note. Having set out his weekly earnings, together with a statement whether or not he has any savings to pay for his defence, at the bottom of the form he has to sign a declaration to the following effect: "I declare that to the best of my knowledge and belief the above particulars are true." Underneath this declaration is printed a warning which runs as follows: "If any person in furnishing this statement of means

After-trial duties — Appeals to Court of Criminal Appeal

knowingly makes any false statement or misrepresentation, he is liable, on summary conviction, to a fine not exceeding one hundred pounds, or imprisonment for a term not exceeding four months, or to both."

It should also be borne in mind that, whilst the Costs in Criminal Cases Act, 1952, places a duty on courts of Assize and Quarter Sessions to allow costs, the provisions of the Act are discretionary and not mandatory. Each case has to be considered on its merits, and as a matter of administrative convenience it is usually the officer of the court who deals with the matters. Solicitors and counsel who feel aggrieved by any assessment have a right to refer the matter to the court, when the judge or chairman will review the position.

Before finally leaving the question of free legal aid, a reference should perhaps be made at this point to the actual sums which have been presented as being payable. These are now contained in the Poor Prisoners' Defence (Defence Certificate) Regulations, 1960, and the Poor Prisoners' Defence (Legal Aid Certificate) Regulations, 1960, as amended by similarly entitled Regulations, 1963.

The scales of payments therein laid down are, as regards solicitors, a fee of not less than £8 8s. 0d. and not exceeding £78 15s. 0d. or, if the trial is not concluded in a day, additional fees for each further day of the hearing.

In addition to the above-mentioned basic fees a solicitor is allowed (*a*) expenses actually and reasonably incurred by himself or his clerk in travelling to and from the court or to any venue necessary for conducting the defence, (*b*) any out-of-pocket expenses actually and reasonably incurred, these being subject to taxation.

Similar provisions apply to solicitors under legal aid certificates on appeals to Quarter Sessions, except that in these cases the fee is not to be less than £6 6s. 0d. and not to exceed £47 5s. 0d. and the fee for an additional days' hearing is not to exceed £9 9s. 0d.

The scale of fees for counsel are also to be found in the Poor Prisoners' Defence (Defence Certificate) Regulations, 1960, and amount to a fee of not less than £8 13s. 0d. and not exceeding £64 10s. 0d. (if two counsel are assigned), such fee as appears proper in all the circumstances of the case.

The regulations further provide both in the case of solicitors and counsel that, if a defence certificate is assigned, either to solicitor or counsel, to represent more than one person, any increases in the fees allowable shall not exceed in respect of a second person 40 per cent of the amount payable but for the increase, and in respect of any other persons 20 per cent of the said amount.

Care has, however, to be taken in determining the amounts to be paid to a solicitor or counsel, that the court takes into account any payment already made in the same case under a legal aid certificate. Since, however, solicitors frequently send their bills of costs to Quarter Sessions and Assizes before the work done at the magistrates' court has been assessed, the clerk of the court, has to be careful to exclude any items prior to committal, or notice of appeal, as the case may be, and also to restrict the fees which he allows for the work done in respect of the hearing at the trial court.

Further work done in connection with giving notice of appeal, or application for leave to appeal, or applying for a case to be stated to the High Court, can be taken into account by an Assize Court or Quarter Sessions. Once, however, an appeal is entered, either in the Court of Criminal Appeal or in the Divisional Court of the High Court, any question of further free aid is no longer the concern of the court of Assize or Quarter Sessions.

The modern tendency is for the courts to make free use of the legal aid system, especially in cases where the defendants plead not guilty. When a defendant on arraignment pleads not guilty to an indictment and is not represented by counsel, it is the almost invariable custom nowadays for the judge or chairman to ask him whether he would like to have the services of counsel.

Should a defendant, when so asked, intimate that he would prefer to conduct his own defence, then he must be allowed to do so, since it would be quite improper for the judge or chairman to force him to be defended by counsel in defiance of his wish to defend himself. Should it transpire after counsel has seen his client that in the interests of the defence it is desirable that witnesses should be called, the judge or chairman will convert the defence into a full legal aid certificate and adjourn the hearing in order that a solicitor also may be assigned to help in the conduct of the defence.

EXAMINATION OF BILLS OF COSTS

As we have already seen, the Costs in Criminal Cases Act, 1952, places a duty on all Assize courts and courts of Quarter Sessions to settle the amount of costs which are to be allowed for the conduct of trials at their courts. Such costs naturally include the fees which are to be allowed to counsel for conducting the prosecution. There is no universal rule on this, but it may not be without interest to note the practice that has been established of recent years in the metropolitan police district in this respect. It is a method which has placed an extra heavy responsibility on the clerk of the court at the Central Criminal Court and on all the respective clerks of the peace in the area. The Bar Council, by agreement with the various clerks, agreed to forego the previously established practice whereby briefs should always be marked before counsel went into court to conduct their cases, the one exception in those days being in the case of prosecutions conducted on behalf of the Director of Public Prosecutions. Certain heads of agreement, relating to minimum fees in respect of pleas of guilty, conference fees, trials of prisoners who pleaded not guilty, etc., were arrived at and the general principles on which fees and refreshers were to be marked were approved.

This agreement cast an extra burden on the clerk of the court at the Central Criminal Court and clerks of the peace, whose duty had been to tax any fees that they considered excessive.

Certainly the Commissioner of Police has been relieved of an invidious task and successfully placed it on the shoulders of the clerks. Taken by and large, the system may be said to be working reasonably well; the truth being that, whoever carries out this particular work, he can never hope to please everybody. Local funds are entitled to be protected, on the one hand, and, on the other hand, counsel are entitled to a reasonable fee for their services.

Before dealing with appeals to the Court of Criminal Appeal it is pertinent to refer shortly to some of the less frequent duties of the clerk of the peace in regard to the examination of costs. Section 242 of the Local Government Act, 1933, as amended by the Local Government Act, 1958, enacts

> On an application made by the council of a county district to the Clerk of the Peace of the county in which the county district is situate, the Clerk of the Peace or his Deputy shall examine any bills of costs incurred by the council in respect of legal business performed on their behalf, and the allowance of any sum on such examination shall be prima facie evidence of the reasonableness of the amount, but not of the legality of the charge.

The section goes on to provide that the clerk of the peace shall be allowed for every such examination such fees as may be fixed by the Master of the Crown Office.

The District Auditor is willing to accept the reasonableness of any such bill of costs when the signed allocatur of the clerk of the peace has been stamped upon it.

This procedure usually applies to bills of costs of a local authority where the clerk is not a solicitor or the work is undertaken by an outside firm.

Though not strictly falling under the heading of costs, another matter which evolves from ancient history is the hearing of occasional applications to Quarter Sessions to vary Corn Rents. These applications take the form of an application to the court to appoint three referees in order to ascertain the average price of a Winchester bushel of good marketable wheat in the county for the last 14 years.

Such applications may be made every 14 years for ever unless the Corn Rents are redeemed, and must be made in the first General Quarter Sessions of the Peace for the county after the Feast of St. Michael the Archangel (i.e. the Michaelmas Quarter Sessions). In effect, nowadays all that the appointed referees (nominated surveyors) have to do is to sign a certificate of the Ministry of Agriculture and Fisheries and produce their report after inquiry at the next Quarter Sessions (the Epiphany Quarter Sessions). Such applications have to be made by counsel.

Another of the ancient duties is the enrolment of appointments of gamekeepers. Section 14 of the Game Act, 1831, empowered the lord of the manor to appoint and depute persons to act as gamekeepers, whilst section 16 of that Act enacted that no such appointment or deputation shall be valid unless registered with the clerk of the peace of the county.

With regard to Quarter Sessions, clerks of the peace are often also clerks to their respective county probation committees, advisory committees, magistrates' courts committees, and in addition hold various other appointments. Since, however, the object of this survey has been to deal with the work of the various criminal courts in this country these other activities which attach to the office of a clerk of the peace are outside the scope of this work.

Enough has been said to show that the matter of dealing with costs has of recent years imposed additional extra work and responsibilities on clerks of assize and clerks of the peace and their staffs. Every payment authorized by the court requires a court order, which has to be duly signed by the appropriate officer and paid on sight by the County Treasurer.

Having now pointed out the various duties which fall on the various clerks after a trial is finally disposed of, and in the event of a conviction, the sentence duly pronounced, we can now turn to the subject of appeals to the Court of Criminal Appeal.

APPEALS TO THE COURT OF CRIMINAL APPEAL

Appeals to the Court of Criminal Appeal are regulated by the Criminal Appeal Rules, 1908, made under the provisions of the Criminal Appeal Act, 1907. A person convicted on indictment may appeal under the provisions of this Act to the Court of Criminal Appeal (*a*) against his conviction on any ground of appeal which involves a question of law alone, (*b*) with the leave of the Court of Criminal Appeal or upon the certificate of the judge who tried him that it is a fit case for appeal, against his conviction on any ground of appeal which involves a question of fact alone, or a question of mixed law and fact, or any other ground which appears to the court to be a sufficient ground of appeal, and (c) with the leave of the Court of Criminal Appeal, against the sentence passed on his conviction, unless the sentence is one fixed by law.

Section 20 extends the provisions of the Act to cover cases where a person is dealt with by Quarter Sessions as a incorrigible rogue under the Vagrancy Act, 1824.

A person against whom an order recommending deportation has been made also has a right of appeal against that order.

A person desiring to appeal should do so within 10 days of the date of his conviction and sentence. This is the reason why the clerk of the court has to retain all exhibits (other than those which are the subject of an order of the court) until this period of time has elapsed since the date of conviction. The Court of Criminal Appeal, however, has power to extend the period within which an appeal may be entered.

The time for appealing against conviction commences to run from the day on which the verdict of the jury was returned. The time for appealing against sentence commences to run from the day on which such sentence was passed by the judge of the court of trial.

A person desiring to appeal against conviction or sentence has to commence his appeal by sending to the registrar of the Court of Criminal Appeal a notice of appeal and should set out the particulars of grounds of appeal, and where a person is in custody he may obtain the necessary forms from the governor of the prison.

Provision is made under section 10 of the Act for the assignment of solicitor and counsel or counsel only to an appellant. The Court of Criminal Appeal may, if it thinks fit, on the application of the appellant admit him to bail pending the determination of his appeal.

It is the duty of the registrar of the Court of Criminal Appeal to take all necessary steps to ensure that all the necessary documents and papers are made available for the proper determination of the appeal or application.

We now turn to the duties of the clerk of the court at which the appellant was convicted, but this is also a suitable time in which to set out the definition of exhibits as defined in the Criminal Appeal Rules, 1908, as amended by the Criminal Appeal Rules, 1960.

The expression "exhibits" is there defined as

> including all books, papers, and documents, and all other property, matters and things whatsoever connected with the proceedings against any person who is entitled or may be authorized to appeal under the Act, if the same have been forwarded to the court of trial on the person accused being committed for trial or have been produced and used in evidence during the trial of, or other proceedings in relation to, a person entitled or authorized under the Act to appeal, and any written statement handed in to the judge of the court of trial by such person, but shall not include the original depositions of witnesses examined before the committing justice or coroner nor any indictment or inquisition against any such person nor any plea filed in the court of trial.

The above definition serves to underline the importance of the duties laid on, first, the clerk to the justices of the committing court, and, secondly, the clerk of the court of trial, to ensure that all the exhibits in a case which are handed over to their charge during the course of the proceedings at either of these courts are carefully preserved with a view to their eventual production, if so required, by the Court of Criminal Appeal. A further point that arises from the definition is the specific exclusion of the original depositions; it is a not unusual occurrence for defending counsel to challenge the accuracy of a witness's memory by putting the original deposition to him in cross-examination, and on occasions attempts have been made to put the original deposition in front of the jury as an exhibit — the definition as now laid down disposes of this possibility.

By section 16 of the Criminal Appeal Act, 1907, shorthand notes are to be taken of the proceedings at the trial of any person on indictment, who, if convicted, is entitled or may be authorized to appeal under that Act. The shorthand note of a trial therefore is a statutory requirement taken at the request of the Court of Criminal Appeal, and a prisoner who desires to appeal may always obtain a full transcript of the trial proceedings at his own expense. In practice, however, in most cases now the transcript is limited to the summing up, antecedents and speeches in mitigation.

The Court of Criminal Appeal has power to call evidence, if they think it necessary or expedient in the interests of justice to do so.

An appellant may abandon an appeal at any time after he has duly served notice of appeal by giving notice of abandonment thereof in the form set out in the rules.

Once an appellant has intimated his desire to abandon an appeal, the Court of Criminal Appeal will allow such notice to be withdrawn only if there are special circumstances, e.g. serious mistake or fraud.

The Court of Criminal Appeal shall allow any appeal against conviction if they think that the verdict of the jury should be set aside on the ground that it is unreasonable or cannot be supported having regard to the evidence, or that the judgment of the court before whom the appellant was convicted should be set aside on the ground of a wrong decision of any question of law, or that on any ground there was a miscarriage of justice, and in any other case shall dismiss the appeal.

There is, however, an important proviso to the above section (4), to the effect that the court may, notwithstanding that they are of opinion that the point raised in the appeal might be decided in favour of the appellant, dismiss the appeal if they consider that no substantial miscarriage of justice has actually occurred.

With regard to appeals against sentence the Court of Criminal Appeal has power to quash the sentence as imposed by the trial court and pass such other sentence warranted in law (whether more or less severe). From time to time sentences are increased by the court.

The provisions of the Criminal Appeal Act, 1964, which came into force on the 10th July 1964 empowers the Court of Criminal Appeal in a case where an appeal against conviction is allowed by reason only of evidence received or available to be received by that Court under section 9 of the Criminal Appeal Act, 1907, and it appears to the Court that the interests of justice so require, the Court may, instead of directing the entry of a judgment and verdict of acquittal as required by section 4 (2) of that Act, order the appellant to be retried.

Section 9 of the Criminal Appeal Act, 1907, enables the Court of Criminal Appeal "to order the production of any document, exhibit or other thing connected with the proceedings, the production of which appears to them necessary for the determination of the case".

In the event of a retrial being ordered, the appellant shall be tried upon a fresh indictment preferred by the direction of the Court of Criminal Appeal, and the retrial will take place before such court as the Court of Criminal Appeal may direct.

On a person who has been ordered to be retried being again convicted on the retrial, the court may order any sentence authorized by law, not being a sentence of greater severity than that passed on the original conviction.

So much for the rights of an appellant in relation to entering and pursuing an appeal from the court of trial to the Court of

Criminal Appeal, and we will now turn to the duties that fall on the clerk of the trial court in this connection. It has already been pointed out that no clerk of a court ought to part with any exhibits in a case, without an order from the court, until the statutory period of 10 days within which a convicted person may enter an appeal from that court has elapsed. It may be noted in passing that there is no statutory time limit for the retention of documents such as the indictment, original depositions and recognizances; the usual practice is to hand them over to the care of the county archivist after a reasonable time has elapsed.

When an appeal is entered, the clerk of the court receives notice from the Registrar of the Court of Criminal Appeal, and he has then to fill in a form which sets out full particulars of the trial. The information that has to be supplied is much the same as is required for the purpose of the after-trial calendar, only somewhat fuller, as in this case the names both of prosecuting counsel and solicitors and of those appearing for the defendant are required to be given. The following documents are required to be sent with the form to the Registrar — or if in any case no such document is available, then reference to that document will be struck out of the form.

(1) Indictment, or memorandum of conviction.
(2) Original depositions.
(3) Copy depositions.
(4) Exhibit list and original exhibits numbered.
(5) Copy exhibit list and copy exhibits numbered.
(6) Notice of additional evidence.
(7) Notice under section 23, Criminal Justice Act, 1948.
(8) Prison department's report.
(9) Antecedents of appellant.
(10) List of previous convictions.
(11) Statement by appellant.
(12) List of offences taken into consideration.
(13) Evidence of medical practitioner taken into account under Section 60 (1) (*a*) of the Mental Health Act, 1959.

After the appeal has been dealt with the form and accompanying documents will be returned to the clerk of the court by the Registrar marked with the result of the appeal.

APPEALS TO THE HOUSE OF LORDS

The final court of appeal in relation to criminal matters in this country is the House of Lords, and it was enacted in the first section of the Administration of Justice Act, 1960, that

> Subject to the provisions of this section, an appeal shall lie to the House of Lords, at the instance of the defendant or the prosecutor, (*a*) from any decision of a Divisional Court of the Queen's Bench Division in a criminal cause or matter; (*b*) from any decision of the Court of Criminal Appeal on an appeal to that court.

It was, however, further enacted that no appeal shall lie, except with the leave of the court below or of the House of Lords and that such leave shall not be granted unless it is certified by the court below that a point of law of general public importance is involved in the decision and it appears to that court or to the House of Lords, as the case may be, that the point is one which ought to be considered by that House.

In Chapter 3, when dealing with the subject of jurors, we had occasion to refer to a recent refusal by the House of Lords to allow an appellant to appeal against the decision of the Court of Criminal Appeal relative to the rights of a defendant as to the challenging by him of jurors (see p. 52).

The above summary of the work that has to be done at all levels by the criminal courts of this country, will I hope, suffice to indicate some of the extra work that has been imposed on them in recent years. One final reflection, however, is worthy of mention, and that is with regard to the lay justices. When one realizes the vast amount of work which is dealt with in the magistrates' courts, and bears in mind that the great majority of such courts are manned by lay justices, it should be remembered that they not only devote much of their time to carrying out their primary duties whilst sitting on the benches of magistrates' courts throughout the realm, but in addition are called on to devote a further portion of their valuable time to carrying out their obligation to sit at Quarter Sessions, both for the purpose of hearing trial cases and also for hearing appeals to Quarter Sessions from their own courts.

A further obligation has now been placed on all justices who have been appointed on or after the 1st January 1966 to undergo a compulsory course of training within the first twelve months from the date of their appointment. All justices appointed on or after that date will also have to undergo a further course of training during the second year after their appointment in order to qualify them for sitting on the bench of a juvenile court.

During the course of one's work at Quarter Sessions one meets many of the lay judiciary, thus enlarging one's circle of friendships. As the years have gone by, the legislature has provided for payments for jurors, witnesses, the defence of poor prisoners, etc., but the lay justice still remains, as he has always been, an unpaid volunteer helping in the administration of justice, except that he has had the benefit of travelling allowances as from the 1st April 1953 and subsistence allowance as from the 22nd June 1964. Many of us who have been connected with Quarter Sessions and magistrates' courts will, I feel sure, hope that this great body of men and women will long remain one of the great pillars of our courts of justice.

APPENDIX I

Recent Statutes affecting Criminal Procedure

THE following statutes have become law during the few months prior to the publication of this manual, and this appendix deals briefly with the main points in which they concern the criminal procedure of our courts. Cross-references are made to the chapters and pages in the main text in order to keep the reader up to date.

The Statutes are as follows:

The Criminal Evidence Act, 1965.
The Criminal Justice Act, 1965.
The Firearms Act, 1965,
The Criminal Procedure (Attendance of Witnesses) Act, 1965.

The Criminal Evidence Act, 1965, came into operation on the 2nd June 1965, the object of the Act being to make certain trade or business records admissible as evidence in criminal proceedings. Where direct oral evidence of a fact would be admissible, any statement contained in a document and tending to establish that fact shall, on production of the document, be admissible as evidence of that fact if:

(*a*) the document is compiled by persons who have, or may reasonably be supposed to have, personal knowledge of the matters dealt with in the information they supply; and
(*b*) the person who supplied the information recorded in the statement in question is dead, or beyond the seas, or unfit by reason of his bodily or mental condition to attend as a witness.

In deciding whether or not a person is fit to attend as a witness, the court may act on a certificate purporting to be a certificate of a fully registered medical practitioner.

The Criminal Justice Act, 1965, which came into force on the 5th September 1965, made provision for the continuation of criminal trials notwithstanding the death or discharge of a juror. Prior to the date on which this Act became operative, a criminal trial could proceed so long as the number of persons on a jury was not reduced below ten (section 15, Criminal Justice Act, 1925). The effect of the 1965 act is to reduce the minimum number from 10 to 9 (see Chapter 3, p. 55). The Act also repeals section 15 of the Criminal Justice Act, 1925, so that written assent on behalf of both the prosecution and the accused is no longer necessary except on a trial for murder or any capital charge.

Sections 1-6 of the Firearms Act, 1965, came into operation on the 5th September 1965 and the remaining sections on the 1st November 1965. The Act amends the Firearms Act, 1937, by introducing new offences as regards trespassing with firearms, conferring powers of search and arrest on constables in connection with firearms, and increasing the penalties both for summary conviction and conviction on indictment in relation to such offences.

The Criminal Procedure (Attendance of Witnesses) Act, 1965, which made a number of important changes of procedure came into force on the 5th October 1965. Section 1 repealed and replaced section 5 of the Magistrates' Courts Act, 1952, thus abolishing the then existing procedure for the binding over of witnesses who have given evidence in committal proceedings (see Chapter 1, p. 11). The effect of this section is that a magistrates' court acting as examining justices is required to make a witness order in respect of each witness examined by the court requiring him to attend and give evidence before the court of trial. Such an order may be conditional if it appears that the presence of the witness at the trial is unnecessary.

Appendix I — Recent Statutes affecting Criminal Procedure

Section 2 provides a new form of process for securing the attendance of a witness before a court of Assize or Quarter Sessions. In this connection the powers of issuing *subpoenas ad testificandum* or *duces tecum* (for the purpose of criminal proceedings) are abolished (section 8). A witness summons may now be issued out of a court of Assize, Quarter Sessions or out of the High Court, requiring a person to whom it is directed to attend before the court and give evidence or produce any document or thing specified in the summons.

The witness summons may be issued by the office of the clerk of assize or clerk of the peace. The person to whom the summons is issued may apply to the court which issued it for it to be set aside. In which case the court if satisfied he cannot give any material evidence may direct that the summons shall be of no effect.

The rules of court in respect of such applications to the High Court will be made under section 99 (4) of the Supreme Court of Judicature (Consolidation) Act, 1925. Schedule 1 of the act lays down the procedure for the making and determination of such applications to a court of Quarter Sessions, and in effect requires that the standing orders of such a court shall make provision (*a*) for requiring the service of notice of any such application on the person at whose instance the witness summons was issued, (*b*) for any such application to be heard and determined otherwise than in court, (i) in the case of quarter sessions for a county or a London commission area, by the chairman or any deputy chairman, (ii) in the case of quarter sessions for a borough, by the Recorder or any deputy or assistant recorder.

Section 3 lays down the punishment for disobedience to a witness order or witness summons. Any person disobeying without just cause shall be guilty of contempt of the court before which he was required to attend, and enacts a maximum period of 3 months' imprisonment, a right of appeal to the appropriate higher court being given by virtue of the provisions of section 13 of the Administration of Justice Act, 1960.

Section 4 empowers a judge of the High Court or a court of Assize or Quarter Sessions before whom a witness has failed to attend in compliance with an order or summons to issue a warrant to arrest him and bring him before the court. Section 5 makes provision for such a warrant to be backed for bail.

By two Statutory instruments (The Poor Prisoners (Counsel and Solicitors) No. 2 Rules, 1965, and the Summary Jurisdiction Appeals (Counsel and Solicitor) Rules, 1965), which came into operation on the 19th July 1965, clerks of the peace are no longer subject to the requirement to keep a list of members of the Bar who are willing to appear as counsel for legally-aided persons (see Chapter 5, p. 120).

The Witnesses' Allowances Regulations 1966 (1966, No. 10) which came into operation on the 14th February 1966 consolidated the earlier Witnesses' Allowances Regulations together with certain minor amendments increasing the subsistence allowances for a witness to 6*s*., 12*s*. 6*d*. and 15*s*. 6*d*. respectively for attendance at court for periods not exceeding 4 or 8 hours and in excess of 8 hours respectively.

The night allowance and seaman's allowance are increased to 50*s*. and slight adjustment is made to travel by a hired vehicle. (See pp. 114, 115.)

As this book goes to press a further Criminal Law Bill is likely to be on the stocks for consideration by Parliament, having as its main objective the abolition of the division of offences into felonies and misdemeanours. The effect of this would be that all offences would be dealt with by the law and practice applicable at the commencement of the proposed Act in relation to misdemeanours. The Bill as at present drafted would not come into force until the 1st September 1966.

APPENDIX II

Dictionary of Prison Slang

a carpet, 3 months.
a case, 5s.
a lay down, 7 days in custody.
a pull, pulled up by police.
a take on, untrue.
belled, fitted with burglar alarm.
bent, stolen or crooked.
bins, binoculars.
bird, jail.
bison, girls.
blister, summons.
blowing the gaff, informing.
boat race, face.
boozer, public house.
brains, C.I.D.
brass, prostitute.
bride, girl friend.
brief, lawyer or solicitor.
bush it, free ride.
casing the joint, reconnaisance.
Charlie Wood, police truncheon.
charred, stolen.
chiv, razor.
chummy, prisoner.
clobber, clothing.
cobblers, lies.
cool, not recently stolen.
cooler, cell.
copped, caught.
dabs, finger prints.
daisy roots, boots.
dicey, chancy.
do a roger, disappear.
dray, vehicle.
driver's bunce, gratuitous.

drum, house.
drumming, housebreaking.
expecting a nick, to be arrested.
fair cop, fair catch.
fence, receiver of stolen property.
finger, name applied to a thief.
flog, to sell.
frog and toad, road.
gaff, eating house.
gear, property.
gelly, gelignite.
gellyman, a man skilled in the use of gelignite.
grass, informer.
gunge, Indian hemp.
grassed, split on (snake in the grass).
handful, 5 years' imprisonment.
have a kip, sleep.
have it away, run away.
heavy mob, Flying Squad officers.
hijack, larceny of goods from a vehicle in transit.
hoch, sell.
hoist, hold up.
hot, recently stolen.
hot drag, recently stolen motor car.
in the middle, no choice but to confess.
jane, girl or bird.
kite, cheque.
load of porridge, prison sentence.
loaf, head.
let the bubble in, squeak (bubble and squeak.)
lumbered, found out.

mouthpiece, counsel.
old lag, prison habitué.
on the floor, skint or broke.
on the knocker, calling from door to door.
on the up and up, straightforward deal.
peter, safe.
peterman, a safe cracker.
pets, girls.
pigeon dove, glove.
pig's ear, beer.
pokey, prison.
poppy, money.
punt, place with a receiver.
punting, placing with a receiver.
rabbiting, talking.
ring, to turn round evidence.
rock, diamond, precious stone.
scram, run.
screw, warder (prison officer).
screwing, housebreaking, shopbreaking, etc., pinching.
scrub, wash out.
skint, broke.
sell the snout, sell stolen property.
slush, forged notes.
snout, tobacco (or informer).
spade, black man.
squeak, to give away.
stack, to dump.
stick, baton.
stretch, term of imprisonment.
strides, trousers.
sweeney tod, Flying Squad.
take it on the toes, run away — estreat recognizance.
take the can back, take the blame.
take the rap, take the blame.
tea leaves, thieves.
the blue, uniformed police officer.
the herberts, thieves.
the johns, copper.
the nick, police station.
toffee, nonsense.
tomfoolery, jewellery.
topped, hung.
to shop, to give away.
to top, to hang.
trap, mouth.
trick cyclist, psychiatrist.
tumbled, understood.
turn grass, become an informer.
twirls, keys.
uncle ned, dead.
wedge, wad of notes.

APPENDIX III

Glossary of Legal Terms in Criminal Law

a fortiori, all the more.

abandonment, not proceeding further, i.e. when an appellant abandons an appeal.

acquittal, found not guilty of a charge.

adjournment, postponement of a hearing to a later date.

affidavit, a statement made in writing on oath.

affirmation, a form which is binding on any person giving evidence who is excused from taking the oath.

alibi, evidence which consists in proving that the accused person was elsewhere than the venue of the crime.

alias, otherwise called.

amendment, a correction.

appeal, the process of trying to get a conviction by a lower court reversed by a higher court.

appellant, the person who enters the appeal.

approved school, a school approved by the Secretary of State under section 79 of the Children and Young Persons Act, 1933.

approved school order, an order made by a court sending a person to an approved school.

arraign, (1) call prisoner by name,
(2) read indictment,
(3) ask prisoner whether guilty or not guilty.

arrears, money due after time for payment has expired.

assessors, lay justices who sit with a Recorder on appeals and committals for release from a juvenile court.

assize court, circuit court for hearing both civil and criminal cases.

attempt, attempt to commit crime.

attendance centre, place selected by Secretary of State to which magistrates' courts may order offenders aged between 12 and 20 years of age to attend.

autrefois acquit, plea when a person previously found not guilty is charged later with the same offence.

autrefois convict, plea in similar circumstances when already convicted of the same offence on an earlier occasion.

142 *The Administration of Criminal Justice in England and Wales*

backing a warrant, endorsement by a justice.
backed for bail, enables police to release on bail after effecting arrest.
bail, release of a person due to appear in court, liable to forfeit a sum of money in default of appearing when called on.
bastard child, a child born out of wedlock.
bench, a tribunal of magistrates or judges.
bench warrant, issued by Quarter Sessions or Assizes in order to effect the arrest of a person who fails to answer to his bail.
bona fide, in good faith.
Borstal, place for the detention of young offenders between the ages of 15 and 21.
breach of peace, any public disturbance.
breach of recognizance, breaking of a condition in a probation order or other court order.
Brewster Sessions, annual sessions of licensing justices.
brothel, place resorted to for prostitution.
burden of proof, duty of proving case.

calendar, list of prisoners awaiting trial at Quarter Sessions or Assizes.
Central Criminal Court, the Assize court for the Greater London Area.
chairman, one who presides at a court.
challenge, right of a prosecutor or defendant to remove a juror from an empanelled jury.
charge, a criminal accusation against a person.
child, a person under the age of 14.
circuit, a division of the kingdom for the purpose of hearing cases at Assizes.
clerk of assize, officer in charge of an assize circuit.
clerk of the peace, officer in charge of Quarter Sessions.
clerk to the justices, officer in charge of magistrates' court.
commission day, the commencing date of an assize.
commission of peace, contains names of justices elected for a commission area.
commitment, sending to prison.
committed for sentence, for incorrigible rogues, Borstal training and under sections 28 and 29 of the Magistrates' Courts Act, 1952.
committal warrant, document signed committing person to prison, detention centre, etc.
common law bind over, requiring a convicted person to enter into recognizances with or without sureties to come up for judgment when called on.
compensation order, an order made by a court ordering an offender to pay damages for injury or compensation for loss.
complaint, means of launching proceedings against a person in a magistrates court.
concurrent sentences, sentences to run at same time.
consecutive sentences, sentences to run on, one following the other.
contempt of court, disregard of authority of courts of justice.
conviction, person confessing to or being found guilty of a crime.

Appendix III — Glossary of Legal Terms in Criminal Law

corrective training, a punishment imposable by courts of Quarter Sessions or Assizes if certain conditions are fulfilled.

corroboration, independent evidence to support principal evidence.

costs, court order ordering payment of sum of money towards costs of prosecution or defence.

counsel, barrister-at-law.

Court of Criminal Appeal, appeal court for cases tried at Quarter Sessions and Assizes.

Court of Oyer and Terminer, Assize court.

courts of Quarter Sessions, courts for hearing cases in any borough or county.

cross-examination, questions put to witness after he has given his evidence in chief.

custos rotulorum, person who has custody of records of sessions.

de facto, actual fact.

de jure, as of right.

defendant, person charged with a misdemeanour.

deposition, evidence of a witness taken down in writing.

detention centre, a place in which persons not less than 14 but under 21 years of age may be kept for short periods under discipline.

discharge — absolute, release generally.
               conditional, release subject to certain conditions.

distringas, writ to distrain on goods and chattels.

dock, place for prisoner when on trial.

embezzlement, offence of intercepting employer's goods or money.

enclosed, a jury considering their verdict in their retiring room.

engrossment, fair copy.

estreat, forfeiture of recognizance.

evidence, matters deposed to on oath.

exhibit, a document or piece of evidence in a trial.

eyre, circuit (assize).

false pretence, a misdemeanour consisting of obtaining goods or money by false statements.

felony, graver crimes (such as murder).

femme sole, single woman.

finding of a jury, verdict of a jury.

fine, monetary punishment.

fit person order, order made by a court committing a juvenile offender to charge of a "fit person".

folio, seventy-two words make up a folio.

forfeiture, compulsory surrender of money or chattels.

forgery, making false document.

gaol delivery, commission enforcing trial of prisoners in gaol.

hearsay evidence, statement of another person proved in evidence by a witness.

highway, a public road.
homicide, *see* **murder** and **manslaughter.**
hospital order, order made by court authorizing admission to and detention in hospital of an offender.
hospital order with restrictions, hospital order made by court of Assize or Quarter Sessions that offender is subject to special restrictions.
hostile witness, a witness who shows hostility to the party calling him.
housebreaking, breaking and entering a house by day.
House of Lords, final appeal court.

imprisonment, a sentence of imprisonment.
in re, in the matter of.
indictment, written accusation at Assizes or Quarter Sessions.
information, means of commencing criminal proceedings in a magistrates' court against a person.
intra vires, within its powers.
ipso facto, by the very fact.

judge, appointed by Lord Chancellor to try cases both civil and criminal.
judgment, sentence or order of court.
jury, body of empanelled jurors to decide facts.
jury bailiff, officer in charge of a jury.
justice of the peace, magistrate.
juvenile court, court for trying charges against children and young persons.
juvenile offenders, persons over 7 and under 18.

larceny, offence of stealing.
locus in quo, place in question.

magistrate, justice of the peace.
malice, intention to do wrongful act.
mandamus, order directed to an inferior court to carry out a certain duty.
manslaughter, unlawful killing without malice.
mens rea, guilty intent.
misdemeanour, offence not amounting to felony.
misdirection, wrong direction on law by judge to jury.
mitigation, address by defending counsel after verdict prior to judgment.
murder, unlawful homicide with malice aforethought.

night, period from 9 p.m. to 6 a.m.
nolle prosequi, a direction by the Attorney-General to stay criminal proceedings.

obiter dictum, a dictum by a judge not essential to decision of case.
oyer and terminer, to hear and determine.

panel, roll of names of jurors.
panel evidence, evidence given by witness on oath.
penalty, punishment.
perjury, wilful giving of false evidence on oath.

Appendix III — Glossary of Legal Terms in Criminal Law

petty sessions, sittings in magistrates' courts.
plea, guilty or not guilty.
precedent, example to be followed.
precept, direction to sheriff for summoning jurors.
preventive detention, sentence on a persistent offender.
prima facie, evidence which is sufficient to support a committal for trial by a magistrates' court, put an accused on his defence or a jury be asked to determine guilt or innocence.
pro rata, proportionately.
probation order, order made in lieu of punishment.
prosecutor, party instituting criminal proceedings.
Public Prosecutor, Director of Public Prosecutions.
putative father, a person adjudged to be the father of a bastard child.

Quarter Sessions, general sessions of the peace.
quash, to make void.

rebuttal, evidence called by prosecution to counter defence evidence.
receiver, a person who receives stolen property.
recognizance, an obligation binding a person under a penalty.
recorder, tries cases at Borough Quarter Sessions.
refresher, additional fee paid to counsel.
remand, recommittal of an accused person to prison.
remand home, place to which juvenile offender is committed to await trial.
res gestae, material facts as opposed to hearsay evidence.
respite, postponement of trial or judgment.
respondent, party opposed to appellants in an appeal.
rider, addition to verdict of a jury.
rogue and vagabond, a person who commits any of the offences for which the offender is to be deemed an idle and disorderly person, having been previously convicted as an idle and disorderly person (Vagrancy Act, 1824, section 4).

sacrilege, breaking into a place of divine worship.
search warrant, warrant to search premises for stolen goods.
sentence — concurrent, judgment of court: two or more sentences to run concurrently.
        consecutive, judgment of court: two or more sentences to run one after the expiration of the first etc.
sheriff, chief officer of a shire.
shrievalty, sheriff's officer.
single woman, spinster.
special verdict, verdict of jury under special directions.
standing orders, orders governing the proceedings of courts of Quarter Session.
stealing, *see* **larceny.**
stipendiary magistrate, full-time paid magistrate.
sub judice, still the subject of litigation.

subpoena ad testificandum, writ directing a person to attend and give evidence.
subpoena duces tecum, writ directing a person to attend and give evidence with documents.
summary conviction, conviction before magistrates.
summing up, charge of judge to jury.
summons, order to a person to appear before magistrates.
surety, a person who agrees to be answerable for another, i.e. agrees to forfeit a sum of money if the other person does not answer bail.

take into consideration, additional offences admitted by accused.
tipstaff, court official.
trial, process of examination before magistrates' or judge and jury.

ultra vires, beyond powers.
uttering, passing off counterfeit coins.

verdict, finding of jury.

warrant, document authorizing arrest of a person (*see also* **committal warrant**).
witness, a person giving evidence on oath.

young person, a person over the age of 14 and under the age of 17.

Table of Statutes

34 Edw. 3, c. 1	Justices of the Peace Act, 1361	1
3 Geo. 4, c. 46	Levy of Fines Act, 1822	110
4 Geo. 4, c. 37	Levy of Fines Act, 1823	110
	Sect. 5	111
5 Geo. 4, c. 83	Vagrancy Act, 1824	118, 122, 128
	Sect. 3	12
	Sect. 4	5, 12, 116
6 Geo. 4, c. 50	Juries Act, 1825	
	Sect. 20	43
1 & 2 Will. 4, c. 32	Game Act, 1831	
	Sect. 14	127
	Sect. 16	127
12 & 13 Vict., c. 45	Quarter Sessions Act, 1849	
	Sect. 11	98
21 & 22 Vict., c. 73	Stipendiary Magistrates Act, 1858	
	Sect. 12	108
22 & 23 Vict., c. 21	Queen's Remembrancer Act, 1859	
	Sect. 32	110
25 & 26 Vict., c. 107	Juries Act, 1862	
	Sect. 12	49
28 & 29 Vict., c. 18	Criminal Procedure Act, 1865	
	Sect. 2	69
35 & 36 Vict., c. 65	Bastardy Laws Amendment Act, 1872	14
	Sect. 4	14
42 & 43 Vict., c. 49	Summary Jurisdiction Act, 1879	96
	Sect. 31	112
49 & 50 Vict., c. 27	Guardianship of Infants Act, 1886	15
55 & 56 Vict., c. 32	Clergy Discipline Act, 1892	42
61 & 62 Vict., c. 15	Criminal Evidence Act, 1898	
	Sect. 1	68
	Sect. 3	69
7 Edw. 7, c. 23	Criminal Appeal Act, 1907	128
	Sect. 4 (2)	131
	Sect. 9	131
	Sect. 10	129
	Sect. 15	76
	Sect. 16	130
	Sect. 20	128

Table of Statutes

8 Edw. 7, c. 15	Costs in Criminal Cases Act, 1908	116
10 Edw. 7 & 1 Geo. 5, c. 24	Licensing (Jurisdiction) Act, 1910	102
1 & 2 Geo. 5, c. 27	Protection of Animals Act, 1911	
	Sect. 2	96
4 & 5 Geo. 5, c. 6	Affiliation Orders Act, 1914	4
5 & 6 Geo. 5, c. 90	Indictments Act, 1915	28, 30
	Sect. 5	87
9 & 10 Geo. 5, c. 71	Sex Disqualification (Removal) Act, 1919	
	Sect. 1	51
10 & 11 Geo. 5, c. 33	Maintenance Orders (Facilities for Enforcement) Act, 1920	15
	Sect. 3	15
	Sect. 4	15
15 & 16 Geo. 5, c. 45	Guardianship of Infants Act, 1925	15
15 & 16 Geo. 5, c. 49	Supreme Court of Judicature (Consolidation) Act, 1925	32
	Sect. 72	32
	Sect. 99 (4)	137
15 & 16 Geo. 5, c. 86	Criminal Justice Act, 1925	
	Sect. 13	72
	Sect. 15	55, 136
20 & 21 Geo. 5, c. 32	Poor Prisoners Defence Act, 1930	119, 122
	Sect. 4	119, 120
23 & 24 Geo. 5, c. 12	Children and Young Persons Act, 1933	13
	Sect. 49	14
23 & 24 Geo. 5, c. 36	Administration of Justice (Miscellaneous Provisions) Act, 1933	30
	Sect. 2	80
	Sect. 2 (1) proviso	31
	Sect. 2 (2)	30
23 & 24 Geo. 5, c. 38	Summary Jurisdiction (Appeals) Act, 1933	96, 115
	Sect. 1	112
	Sect. 2	80, 97
	Sect. (2) (1)	121
	Sect. 2 (3)	121
	Sect. 3	95, 97
	Sect. 7	95
23 & 24 Geo. 5, c. 51	Local Government Act, 1933	
	Sect. 242	126
1 Edw. 8 & 1 Geo. 6, c. 12	Firearms Act, 1937	136
1 & 2 Geo. 6, c. 63	Administration of Justice (Miscellaneous Provisions) Act, 1938	
	Sect. 3 (1)	104
8 & 9 Geo. 6, c. 41	Family Allowances Act, 1945	
	Sect. 4 (3)	15
9 & 10 Geo. 6, c. 81	National Insurance Act, 1946	16
	Sect. 19 (2)	16

Table of Statutes

11 & 12 Geo. 6, c. 26	Local Government Act, 1948	101
11 & 12 Geo. 6, c. 58	Criminal Justice Act, 1948	25, 82, 84, 91, 99, 109
	Sect. 8	89
	Sect. 14	109, 110
	Sect. 15	109
	Sect. 17	92
	Sect. 18	92
	Sect. 20	25, 91
	Sect. 20 (5) (a) (ii)	26
	Sect. 20 (5) (d)	26
	Sect. 21	82
	Sect. 21 (1)	83
	Sect. 21 (2)	83
	Sect. 22	82
	Sect. 23	27, 64, 132
	Sect. 29	26, 91
	Sect. 29 (5)	84
	Sect. 35	50
	Sect. 35 (1)	51
	Sect. 44	116
	Sect. 53	42
	Ninth Schedule	112, 113
12, 13 & 14 Geo. 6, c. 27	Juries Act, 1949	
	Sect. 1	60
	Sect. 1 (1) proviso	61
	Sect. 2	60
	Sect. 3	61
	Sect. 7	61
12, 13 & 14 Geo. 6, c. 33	Consolidation (Procedure) Act, 1949	116
12, 13 & 14 Geo. 6, c. 51	Legal Aid and Advice Act, 1949	122
	Sect. 18 (2)	119
	Sect. 18 (3)	120
	Sect. 18 (4)	122
	Sect. 23	122
12, 13 & 14 Geo. 6, c. 76	Marriage Act, 1949	
	Sect. 3	16
12, 13 & 14 Geo. 6, c. 99	Summary Jurisdiction (Separation and Maintenance) Acts, 1895 to 1949	15
12, 13 & 14 Geo. 6, c. 101	Justices of the Peace Act, 1949	3, 4
	Sect. 13	85
15 & 16 Geo. 6 & 1 Eliz. 2, c. 48	Costs in Criminal Cases Act, 1952	115, 116, 122, 123, 125
	Sect. 1	116, 117
	Sect. 1 (2)	116, 118
	Sect. 2	117
	Sect. 6	117

Costs in Criminal Cases Act, 1952 (*cont.*)
      Sect. 7 117
      Sect. 8 117
      Sect. 9 117
      Sect. 10 117
      Sect. 11 117
      Sect. 12 117
      Sect. 14 117
      Sect. 17 118

15 & 16 Geo. 6 & 1 Eliz. 2, c. 55 Magistrates' Courts Act, 1952 3, 91, 99
      Sect. 5 11, 72, 136
      Sect. 9 (1) (a) 22
      Sect. 10 (2) 22
      Sect. 12 79
      Sect. 18 (1) 9
      Sect. 18 (3) 10, 26
      Sect. 18 (5) 10
      Sect. 19 10, 26
      Sect. 27 12
      Sect. 27 (3) 5
      Sect. 28 10, 22, 25, 26, 78, 91, 93, 94, 96, 118
      Sect. 29 10, 11, 22, 26, 78, 84, 91, 93, 96, 97, 118
      Sect. 52 4
      Sect. 58 16
      Sect. 83 96
      Sect. 83 (3) 96
      Sect. 84 98, 99
      Sect. 85 97
      Sect. 87 (4) 98
      Sect. 89 96
      Sect. 98 4
      Sect. 125 9
      Sixth Schedule 113

1 & 2 Eliz. 2, c. 46 Licensing Act, 1953 17, 101, 102, 103
      Sect. 2 (2) 101
      Sect. 18 (1) (a) 103

2 & 3 Eliz. 2, c. 41 Juries Act, 1954 61

5 & 6 Eliz. 2, c. 29 Magistrates' Courts Act, 1957 5
      Sect. 3 5

5 & 6 Eliz. 2, c. 55 Affiliation Proceedings Act, 1957
      Sect. 1 17

6 & 7 Eliz. 2, c. 31 First Offenders Act, 1958 9

6 & 7 Eliz. 2, c. 55 Local Government Act, 1958 126

7 & 8 Eliz. 2, c. 25 Highways Act, 1959 101

7 & 8 Eliz. 2, c. 72 Mental Health Act, 1959
      Sect. 60 (1) (a) 132

Table of Statutes

8 & 9 Eliz. 2, c. 16	Road Traffic Act, 1960	
	Sect. 105	100
	Sect. 106	88
8 & 9 Eliz. 2, c. 48	Matrimonial Proceedings (Magistrates' Courts) Act, 1960	
	Sect. 2	17
8 & 9 Eliz. 2, c. 60	Betting and Gaming Act, 1960	99, 101
8 & 9 Eliz. 2, c. 65	Administration of Justice Act, 1960	133
	Sect. 1	133
	Sect. 13	137
9 & 10 Eliz. 2, c. 39	Criminal Justice Act, 1961	10, 25, 82, 93
	Sect. 1	92
	Sect. 2	92
	Sect. 2 (2)	92
	Sect. 3	92
	Sect. 4	92
	Sect. 5	92
	Sect. 6	92
	Sect. 7	92
9 & 10 Eliz. 2, c. 61	Licensing Act, 1961	101, 102
	Sect. 12	19, 102
10 & 11 Eliz. 2, c. 15	Criminal Justice Administration Act, 1962	25
	Sect. 4 (1)	33
	Sect. 4 (5)	86
	Sect. 4 (6)	95
	Sect. 4 (7)	95
	Sect. 14	117
	Sect. 17	78
	Sect. 17 (1)	108
	Sect. 17 (2)	108
	Sect. 18	118
10 & 11 Eliz. 2, c. 21	Commonwealth Immigration Act, 1962	64, 122
10 & 11 Eliz. 2, c. 59	Road Traffic Act, 1962	
	Sect. 6	88
1963 c. 2	Betting, Gaming and Lotteries Act, 1963	101
	Sect. 2	19
1963 c. 37	Children and Young Persons Act, 1963	13
	Sect. 8	107
	Sect. 9	107
	Sect. 16	64
	Sect. 28	14
1964 c. 26	Licensing Act, 1964	
	Sect. 7	18
	Sect. 12 (3)	18
	Sect. 12 (4)	18
1964 c. 34	Criminal Procedure (Right of Reply) Act, 1964	69

Table of Statutes

1964 c. 42	Administration of Justice Act, 1964 33, 85
	Schedule 1 32, 85
1964 c. 43	Criminal Appeal Act, 1964 131
1964 c. 84	Criminal Procedure (Insanity) Act, 1964 58
1965 c. 20	Criminal Evidence Act, 1965 135
1965 c. 26	Criminal Justice Act, 1965 55, 135, 136
1965 c. 44	Firearms Act, 1965 135
	Sect. 1 136
	Sect. 2 136
	Sect. 3 136
	Sect. 4 136
	Sect. 5 136
	Sect. 6 136
1965 c. 69	Criminal Procedure (Attendance of Witnesses) Act, 1965 135, 136
	Sect. 1 136
	Sect. 2 137
	Sect. 3 137
	Sect. 4 138
	Sect. 5 138
	Sect. 8 137
	Schedule 1 137

Index

Additional cases taken into consideration 80
Adjournments 55, 70–2, 104
Administration of Justice Act, 1960 133, 137
Administration of Justice Act, 1964 33, 85
Administration of Justice (Miscellaneous Provisions) Act, 1933 30, 31, 80
Administration of Justice (Miscellaneous Provisions) Act, 1938 104
Affiliation 17
Affiliation orders 14
Affiliation Orders Act, 1914 4
Affiliation Proceedings Act, 1947 17
After-trial calendar 112
After-trial duties 104–34
Appeal aid certificate 115
Appeal Aid Certificate Rules, 1960 115
Appeals 25, 26, 27, 38, 57, 69, 81
 from magistrates' courts 95–101
 notification of results of 112
 right of xiii, xx, 6
 to Court of Criminal Appeal 128–32
 to House of Lords 133–4
 to Quarter Sessions 106, 108
Appellate jurisdiction xiii
Applications to court 87
Approved school 106–7
Archbold's *Criminal Pleading, Evidence and Practice* xx
Assessors, appointment of 42

Assize Courts xix, xx
 additional cases taken into consideration 80
 adjournments 70–2
 applications to court 87
 arrangement of lists 34–8
 calendar compilation 39
 commital for trial 22
 comparison with Quarter Sessions xxi
 costs 116–19
 examination of bills of costs 125–7
 fines imposed and estreated recognizances 109
 fixing of dates 32
 judgment 77
 legal aid certificates 119–25
 matters dealt with by xxiii
 pleas of guilty 64
 pleas of not guilty 66
 precept 44
 proclamation 72
 sentencing 108
 transition from magistrates' courts to 22–42

Bail 12, 70–1, 100
Bail estreats 79
Baines Act 98
Bastardy Laws Amendment Act, 1872 14
Bench warrant 79
Betting and Gaming Act, 1960 99, 101
Betting, Gaming and Lotteries Act, 1963 19, 101
Betting office licences 39

Index

Betting office permits 19
Bookmakers' permits 19, 39
Borstal 10–11, 26, 65, 92, 93
Breaches of probation orders and conditional discharges 89

Calendar compilation 39
Central Criminal Court 37, 70
  sessions 32
Children 13
  custody of 16
  guardianship of 16
Children and Young Persons Acts, 1933 to 1963 13, 14, 64, 107
Civil debts, recovery of 20
Clergy Discipline Act, 1892 42
Commission Day 40
Committal for sentence x, 10, 25, 36, 91–5
Committal for trial 11, 22
Committal warrants 105–9
Commonwealth Immigrants Act, 1952 64
Commonwealth Immigrants Act, 1962 122
Conditional discharge 89
Consolidation of (Procedure) Act, 1949 116
Corn Rents 126
Corrective training 82
Costs
  examination of bills of 125–7
  in criminal cases 116–19
  in Criminal Cases Act, 1908 116
  in Criminal Cases Act, 1952 116, 122, 123, 125
Counsel's fees 125
County Compensation Committee 42, 102–3
County Confirming and Compensation Committee 102
County Days 33, 41, 84
County Licensing Committee 102
Court Expenses (Recovery) Regulations, 1963 118

Court of Criminal Appeal xx, xxiii, 26, 51, 57–9, 69–77, 81, 83, 89, 90
  appeals to 128–32
Criminal Appeal Act, 1907 76, 128, 130, 131
Criminal Appeal Act, 1964 131
Criminal Appeal Rules, 1908 75, 128, 129
Criminal Appeal Rules, 1960 129
Criminal Cases Act, 1952 116, 118
Criminal Evidence Act, 1898 68, 69
Criminal Evidence Act, 1965 135–6
Criminal Justice Act, 1925 55, 72, 136
Criminal Justice Act, 1948 xv, 25, 26, 27, 42, 50, 51, 64, 82, 84, 89, 91, 92, 99, 109–13, 116
Criminal Justice Act, 1961 10, 25, 82, 92
Criminal Justice Act, 1962 25, 86, 108, 118
Criminal Justice Administration Act, 1962 78, 95, 117
Criminal Procedure Act, 1865 69
Criminal Procedure (Attendance of Witnesses) Act, 1965 136
Criminal Procedure (Insanity) Act, 1964 58
Criminal Procedure (Right of Reply) Act, 1964 69
Curative treatment xi
Custody of children 16
Custos rotulorum 1

Defence certificate 119–25
Depositions xx, 23, 74
Detention centres xii, 65, 92
Dock brief 121
Domestic proceedings 15

Easter Quarter Sessions 42
Epiphany Quarter Sessions 42, 103, 127
Estreat roll 109–11
Exhibits 23–4, 55, 75–7, 129

Index

False pretences   29
Felony   66, 67
Fines   109–11
  recovery of   110
Firearms Act, 1937   136
Firearms Act, 1965   136
First offender   9
First Offenders Act, 1958   9

Game Act, 1831   127
Gamekeepers, enrolment of appointments of   127
Guardianship of children   16

High Court of Justice, matters dealt with by   xxiii
Highway applications   101
Highways Act, 1959   101
House of Lords   xxiii
  appeals to   133–4

Idle and disorderly persons   12
Incorrigible rogues   12, 128
Indecent exposure   xi
Indictable offence   9
Indictment   28–31, 71
  application to amend   67
Indictments Act, 1915   28, 30, 87
Indictments Rules   30
Insanity of accused   58
Intermediate Sessions   33, 84
Interpreter, payment of   115

"Judges' Rules"   viii
Judgment   77
Juries Act, 1825   43
Juries Act, 1949   60, 61
Juries Act, 1954   61
Jurors   34, 43–62
  administering the oath   52
  age limit of   59
  calling of   47
  challenge of   50, 67
  discharge of   56
  duties of   ix
  empanelling of   x, 45, 47–9
  illness during adjournment   55
  payment of   59, 113–16
  penalty for non-appearance   49
  right to challenge   x
  see also Jury
Juror's Allowance Regulations   61
Jury   ix
  communications to judge or chairman   55
  disagreements   59
  empanelling of   x, 45, 47–9
  incomplete   55–6
  putting in charge   52
  reduction to seven   59
  taking of verdict   56
  verdict of   53, 70
  see also Jurors
Jury bailiff   53, 55
Jury cards   48
Jury excuses   46–8, 59
Jury service, exemptions   46
Jury summons   49
Justices, appointment of   42
Justices' clerks
  appointment of   3
  duties of   4
Justices' licence   17, 101–3
Justices of the Peace   1
Justices of the Peace Act, 1949   3, 4, 85
Justices of the Peace (Size and Chairmanship of Bench) Rules, 1950   2, 85
Justices (Supplemental List) Rules, 1950   2
Juvenile court   2, 13–14, 107
  matters dealt with by   xxiii
Juvenile delinquents   36
Juvenile panel   2

Larceny   58, 59
Legal Aid and Advice Act, 1949   119, 120, 122
Legal aid certificates   119–25
Legal terms   141

Index

Levy of Fines Acts, 1822 and 1823 110
Licensing 17, 101–3
Licensing Act, 1910 102
Licensing Act, 1953 17, 101, 102, 103
Licensing Act, 1961 19, 101, 102
Licensing Act, 1964 18
Licensing committee 101
Licensing justices 17
Local Government Act, 1933 126
Local Government Act, 1948 101
Local Government Act, 1958 126

Magistrates
  appointment of 1
  instruction of 87
  stipendiary 3
Magistrates' courts xix, 1–21, 136
  affiliation 17
  affiliation orders 14
  appeals from 95–101
  appeals to Quarter Sessions 38–9, 106, 108
  appointment of magistrates 1
  bookmakers' and betting office permits 19
  breaches of probation orders 91
  civil debts, recovery of 20
  committal for sentence x, 10, 25, 36, 91–5
  committal for trial 11, 22
  criminal jurisdiction 3
  domestic proceedings 15
  hearing of 7
  justices' clerk 3
  licensing 17
  matters dealt with by xxiii
  offence triable either on indictment or summarily 9
  plea of guilty without attending court 5
  power of adjournment 7
  restrictions as to powers of imposing imprisonment 8–9
  size of bench 2
  summary offence 9
  summary trial 4
  transition to Quarter Sessions and Assize Courts 22–42
  trial of information 6
  vagrancy 12
  work of xix
Magistrates' Courts Act, 1952 3–5, 9, 10, 16, 22, 25, 26, 72, 78, 79, 84, 91, 93, 96–9, 113, 118, 136
Magistrates' Courts Act, 1957 5
Magistrates' Courts Committee 4
Magistrates' Courts Rules 3, 4, 72, 74
Matrimonial proceedings 17
Matrimonial Proceedings Act, 1960 17
Medical reports 83
Michaelmas Quarter Sessions 41–2, 127
Middlesex Quarter Sessions, case statistics xvii
Motoring offences 88, 100, 101

Newspaper reporting, restrictions on 16
Nolle prosequi 31

Occasional licences 18
Opening Proclamation 84

Persistent offenders 82
Pleas of guilty 5, 64, 95
  without attending court 5
Pleas of not guilty 66
Police caution viii
Poor Prisoners (Counsel and Solicitor) Rules, 1931 120
Poor Prisoners (Counsel and Solicitors) No. 2 Rules, 1965 138
Poor Prisoners' Defence Act, 1930 119–20, 122
Poor Prisoners' Defence (Defence Certificate) Regulations, 1960 123

Index

Poor Prisoners' Defence (Legal Aid Certificate) Regulations, 1960 and 1963 123
Precept 44
Preventive detention 82
Prison Rules, 1949 42
Prison slang 139
Probation officers' reports 83, 90
Probation orders 107
  breach of 89
Proclamation 72

Quarter Sessions xiii, xix, xx, 63–103
  additional cases taken into consideration 80
  adjournments 70–2
  appeals from magistrates' courts 38–9, 95–101
  appeals to 106, 108
  applications to court 87
  arrangement of lists 34–8
  breaches of probation orders and conditional discharges 89
  calendar compilation 39
  committal for sentence x, 10, 25, 36, 91–5
  committal for trial 11, 22
  comparison with Assizes xxi
  costs 116–19
  county day agenda 41
  examination of bills of costs 125–7
  fines imposed and estreated recognizances 109
  fixing of dates 33
  judgment 77
  legal aid certificates 119–25
  licensing 101–3
  matters dealt with by xxiii
  opening proclamation 84
  pleas of guilty 64
  pleas of not guilty 66
  precept 44
  rota of justices 85
  sentencing 108
  size of bench 84–5
  Standing Orders 41
  times of sitting 84
  transition from Magistrates' Courts to 22–42
Quarter Sessions Act, 1849 98
Queen's Remembrancer Act, 1859 110

Rating assessments 101
Receiving 58, 59
Recognizances 108
Road Traffic Act, 1960 88, 100
Road Traffic Act, 1962 88
Rogues and vagabonds 12, 122

Sentence
  committal for *see* Committal
  variation during Assizes or Sessions 66
Sentencing xi, xii, 78, 82, 108
Sex Disqualification (Removal) Act, 1919 51
Sheriff, duties of 44–5, 46, 49, 111
Shoplifting xi
Statutes affecting criminal procedure 135–8
Statutory Rules and Regulations xvii
Stipendiary Magistrates' Act, 1958 108
Stone's *Justices Manual* xx
Subpoena ad testificandum 137
Subpoena duces tecum 137
Summary Jurisdiction Act, 1879 96, 112
Summary Jurisdiction (Appeals) Act, 1933 95, 96, 112, 121
Summary Jurisdiction Appeals (Counsel and Solicitor) Rules, 1965 138
Summary offence 9
Summary trial 4
Summing up 70
Supreme Court of Judicature (Consolidation) Act, 1925 137

Surety 70

Transfer licence 18
Treason 67
Trial by jury 43, 63–103
   procedure 67
"Trial within a trial" ix

Under-sheriff, duties of 45
Unsworn statement 68

Vagrancy 12
Vagrancy Act, 1824 5, 12, 116, 118, 122, 128
Verdict 53, 70
   failure to agree on 54
   special 57–8
   taking of 56
Visiting Committees 42

Witnesses ix, 23, 65–9, 72–5, 136
   additional 73
   bound over 72
   conditionally bound over 72, 73
   payment of 113–16
   procedure for ensuring attendance 74
   punishment for disobedience to order or summons 137
   securing attendance of 137
Witnesses' Allowances Regulations 113

Young offenders x, 92
Young persons 13, 64, 65, 107